PUNCHING HOLES in the DARKNESS

Ida Nelle Hollaway

Broadman Press
Nashville, Tennessee

To Ernest,
who shared all the commitment, joy,
and pain of these last thirty-six
years, and
To Mother,
Mrs. Flora Whitwell Daily, who "held
the ropes" at home in constant prayer.

© Copyright 1978 ● Broadman Press.
All rights reserved.
4255-87
ISBN: 0-8054-5587-6

Dewey Decimal Classification: 266.52
Subject Heading: MISSIONS—JAPAN
Library of Congress Catalog Card Number: 77-81521
Printed in the United States of America

Preface

Very few experiences in all of my life are etched as deeply on my heart as the spiritual need in Japan and the memory of my friends there.

I have told some of the circumstances of our return to America in my first Broadman book, *When All the Bridges Are Down.* I am not sure I will ever come to the place where I do not feel that perhaps God's *perfect* will for our lives would have been to live them out in Japan, had I been able to handle things a little differently. Else, I ponder, why did he give Ernest such an unusual gift with the language and me such a burdened heart for the people?

However, not long ago my pastor, Bob Norman, reminded us, "God doesn't will *everything* in our lives, but he *does* will something *in* everything in our lives."

I feel very strongly that at least part of his will *in* our return is that I share with as many people as possible the great challenge I found there. The many, many Japanese stories recorded here are given with a deeply sincere prayer that you may come to know these people, love them, and feel their need. There is also a prayer that you may hear the Savior's plea, "I have other sheep, that are not of this fold" (John 10:16, RSV); "feed my lambs" (John 21:15, RSV).

Mrs. R. L. Mathis, when president of the Woman's Missionary Union, was the first to suggest that I put these stories in print. They have been a long time coming, but the burden is as intense as ever.

Some people have tried to discourage me into thinking that Americans are not as interested in foreign fields these days. I am so grateful that God gave me a publisher, Broadman, which has the vision to see that, though people may tire of facts and figures, people still love people and care what happens to them. I still believe that there are a large number of intensely Christian people who would like to see the church take more seriously our Savior's last command.

IDA NELLE HOLLAWAY

Nashville, Tennessee

Contents

1.
The Call of the Darkness

I sat staring at the headline. Both the Japanese and English papers carried it. "Young Couple Die in Suicide Pact."

I read it for perhaps the tenth time. Through my tears I kept trying to absorb all it meant. The story was brutally clear.

Two promising, intelligent university students had fallen deeply in love. They had hoped to be married. But, being obedient Japanese young people, they followed the traditional custom of asking permission from both of their families. This permission was promptly denied.

It seemed the girl had royal blood in her veins and the boy's family were commoners. Either family would have been greatly embarrassed by the union.

The two talked it over at great length. They waited quite awhile, hoping to work something out. Finally they decided to run away to the Amagi Mountains south of Tokyo and consummate their love without the benefit of marriage.

Once in the mountains, they rented a room in a little mountain inn. But they could not bring themselves to lower the standards they had cherished. They felt it would tarnish their love to carry out their plan.

They saw only one solution. If they could not live

together, they would die together. They bought the medicine they planned to take and made their preparations to commit suicide.

They decided to spend one last day together, wandering through the beautiful Amagi mountains, before they died.

Our Japanese Christians have a summer encampment ground in this very area, which they call *Amagi Sanso* (gateway to heaven). At the entrance to that assembly ground some of the Japanese Christians had found a crystal-clear mountain spring. They walled it up with the native stone into an everflowing fountain for thirsty passersby.

In the mountain stone above the fountain they carved these words of Scripture: "Everyone who drinks of this water will thirst again, but whoever drinks of the water that I shall give him will never thirst; the water that I shall give him will become in him a spring of water welling up to eternal life" (John 4:13-14, RSV).

This young couple, on their last walk through the mountains, had come to this fountain. They had stood for a long while reading the words and wondering what they meant. Then they had gone back to their hotel to die.

As I read the account, this was the part which really brought the tears. The last thing the girl had done on this earth was to write in her diary. In it she told of their frustration and despair, of their decision and their final walk together. She described the fountain and the words carved over it. One of the last things she wrote was "What could it have meant, 'spring of water . . . to eternal life'?"

I sat and wept, but I was not just weeping for the young suicides. We had known many of them. I was

8

weeping for the millions and millions of young people across Japan who would read that account that day and in their own frustrations and deep needs would ask futilely, "What *could* it have meant, 'spring of water . . . to eternal life'?"

All of the facts—the terrible, disturbing, challenging facts we lived with every day—came tumbling through my mind. Facts about the nature of the spiritual need about us, the darkness. Many Christians I have met, before and since, have wanted to turn from the use of the word *darkness* as a description of their condition. But my own experience has brought me to a firm conviction of the truth of the Scripture, "God is light, and in him is no darkness at all" (1 John 1:5, KJV). I believe, too, that life without him is darkness. All I have seen of the way those without him face eternity or the trials of this life bears this out. I was never surprised to learn that Tokyo was the suicide capital of the world.

To understand this darkness, I had only to imagine trying to face one year, one month, even one day without Christ. But here, in this land to which God had brought us, only 1/2 of 1 percent of the people knew Christ. This meant that 99½ percent of the people were having to face all of the tragedies, all of the uncertainties, all of the fears of their lives without the love and light of God.

As I sat there with the morning paper, weeping, this sense of darkness seemed to engulf me. Still, it was because of this darkness that we had come. I remembered vividly the struggles in my own heart the day we had left our homeland.

How reluctant I had felt to let go of the crepe-paper streamers that still connected us to the shore. Since I had never been on a large ocean liner before, I had not been aware of this custom until then. The ship had been cleared of all visitors; the gangplanks were up; and most of the passengers for the two-week voyage were out on the main deck to say good-bye to America. We were given rolls of streamers we could throw to waiting relatives and friends on the pier below.

We had never been very close to the California relatives who came to see us off, but suddenly they became symbolic of all those we loved and were leaving. Unlike most of the passengers, we were not saying good-bye for two weeks or so of vacation. We would not see this shore again for five years. The fragile streamer became the last connection between us and the land we loved. I held it tightly and dreaded to see it break as we moved slowly away from the dock.

I am certain that many others were feeling this, for a quietness settled over the group as we moved away.

Finally the people on the pier put down their broken ends of the streamers, ceased to call or wave, and gradually left. As we looked at the damp pier, covered with fallen, soggy streamers, our older son Lee, then six, broke the tension with his comment, "Boy, that pier sure looks celebrated!"

It was late afternoon, and a great number of passengers who were on pleasure trips and vacation cruises soon became boisterous and hurried below for predinner cocktails. We lingered on the main deck. While our boys explored their new surroundings, we stood in silence, reflecting on the deep meaning of the moment.

Almost two decades before, as a child, I had first heard some missionary use the phrase "sailing into the sunset." It had sounded romantic and exciting. Through the years it had come to mean to me something of ultimate surrender, to be able to leave the familiar, loved things and go out into the unknown for God. Standing on the quiet deck, the romanticism became hard reality.

I kept seeing the faces of our parents, who found it hard to accept the meaning of the five years of separation from their grandchildren. Bill, just turned five, and Lee, soon to be seven, seemed so delightful and loving to them. What would they be like, they wondered, when they came back as energetic boys of ten and twelve?

My parents had recently acquired the home they had dreamed about for thirty-five years. Its rolling acres and ponds and horses were perfect for grandchildren. But now two of their three, and the only ones old enough to enjoy those surroundings, were going away.

Ernest's mother had just had a serious bout with cancer, and the usual five years' waiting period before the extent of cure could be ascertained meant even more than the usual frustration to her. If she didn't make the five years, she would never see her only child and grandchildren again. I am glad that none of us knew at the time that she had only a year and a half left.

I kept my eyes on the American flag floating above some building near the dock. It had never meant more to me. My patriotism had never been of an overly sentimental nature, but at that moment I wished I could hear someone playing "America" or "The Star-Spangled Banner." I wondered how long it would be before I would again stand in a group with hands across our breasts, saluting that flag. I wondered, too, how much allegiance I would grow to feel for the flag of my new land. In my mind I could see that large red circle on a field of white, the flag of the land of the rising sun, Japan. It was a symbol that had so recently spelled

11

infamy in our country.

It still had not been quite four years since the war between our two countries had ended. My only brother, a doctor, had spent three years on a regimental combat team in the Pacific, participating in invasion after invasion. The three doctors he lived with and worked with had been picked off one by one by Japanese snipers until only he was left. He had to dig in the underground to operate to keep the snipers from shooting his patients on the operating table.

For three years I had lived in fear of his death by Japanese hands. It had never occurred to me during those days that these were the people I would be going to live with and share with under their flag.

The decision had not come quickly. It had taken us twelve years from the time of volunteering for missions to reach our appointment by our Foreign Mission Board. We had four years of college, four years of military service, and four years of seminary. When we finally reached the Board our original target area, Europe, had an overbalance of volunteers. Our original aim in volunteering had been to go to the place of greatest need, so we just asked the personnel at the Mission Board to suggest the neediest place our particular qualifications seemed to fit. They suggested Japan. They said we only had twelve missionaries still under appointment for Japan at the close of the war. They hoped to increase this number to at least one hundred as soon as possible. This suited us just fine; so we were appointed immediately, with very little knowledge of the country or its people.

Now, as I watched our flag disappearing in the distance and thought about the Japanese flag with its lone red sun, I thought of the silk flag my brother, Bill, had brought home from the war. It had been taken from the body of a Japanese soldier. Almost every soldier had one, he had said. On the white field around the sun were dozens of signatures of friends and loved ones who were thinking of the soldier, wishing him well, praying for him, loving him.

As I stood on the deck that evening I thought of that flag and of all those who had loved their soldiers, who had ached and waited for their fallen loved ones, just as we had done. Yet I knew that they had to face their anguish and their loss without our Comforter. In that moment, once again, the sense of this darkness had brought my sense of mission back into focus and had helped me to turn from watching the last lights of my homeland in the distance. I went below to begin the voyage.

We enjoyed the trip. Two other missionary couples and three single missionaries, who were also being sent to Japan by our Mission Board, sailed with us. We shared happy hours with them, made many new friends, and enjoyed all of the wonderful facilities for relaxing and vacationing. We didn't spend too many mornings down in our stateroom fighting nausea. The children were very intrigued with the ship, the large playroom, the separate dining room for children where they could order their own meals without parental help, and the salt-water swimming pool.

I spent a lot of time just sitting in a deck chair, thinking. We had been so busy in all the rush of finishing school, selling our house, packing, speaking in churches, and paying farewell visits to families that there had been little time to think. Now all those thoughts and questions came flooding in.

Of course, we had many questions about our new land, its people, and the language study ahead; but more of my thoughts centered around our two children. They were at our mercy. And we had chosen to uproot them, sever connections with their families and friends, and put them into a new and strange environment. How would they fare? What would Lee's new school be like? How was he to get across the largest city in the world each day? Would Bill be able to go to kindergarten? Who would care for him the several hours a day Ernest and I would be in Japanese language school?

However, as I watched the two of them playing with their American friends on board ship, another, deeper question formed in my mind. As I watched them, so open, friendly, uninhibited, and happy, I wondered what the next five years would do to them. Would they fit this well into a group of American kids then? Would they become strange, in some way foreign, less at ease in their own culture?

I think the first relief I had from this nagging questioning came when we docked in Yokohama. Bob Sherer, an Alabama missionary, and his young son, Bobby, came to meet our ship. Bobby was just slightly younger than our Bill, and he was delightful. He couldn't have looked more like a happy, well-adjusted, mischievous American kid. His grin was just as infectious as Bill's, and he was ready immediately to join our boys in exploring, running, and joking. My heart was singing, *Nothing seems to be bothering him!*

Once off the ship our apprehensions began to return. We were thrown immediately into heavy, unending traffic. This was not traffic as I had known it. It was more a traffic of people than vehicles. People walked in the

14

streets and rode bicycles, carrying great loads. Ten trays of food might be held high in one hand while the other hand tried to steer a bicycle through the traffic. The only motorized vehicles were little three-wheeled carts, piled high with merchandise. Great charcoal-burning trucks drove wildly through the crowds with their horns blowing constantly. I thought I had never seen so many people. I had the feeling that we must be very near a large fairground that had just turned its people out. But the sensation did not end. It went on for miles and miles.

When we had finally covered the distance between Yokohama and Tokyo and came nearer to the place we were to live, my heart sank. The crowds seemed to be increasing. We were to live, we found, in one of the busiest districts of crowded Tokyo. Even the alley into our mission compound was filled with people. I was already worrying about the children and what their reaction would be. I should not have done so. Bill's next excited remark made that evident:

"Oh, Lee! Look at all the friends we haven't met yet!"

His insight proved prophetic. We were amazed at the friendly acceptance we experienced among the Japanese people.

It is hard to explain how deeply we felt drawn to them from the very beginning. Many of their innate qualities brought this immediate response, and it increased as the years went by. One of the strongest of these was their love for children, ours as well as their own. How often I sat in their parks, intrigued as I watched busy parents taking time to respond patiently and skillfully to every discovery of their child—blades of grass, smooth pebbles, small worms or snails. Perhaps this reflects another attitude which drew us to them: their great love for nature

15

and their ability to enjoy even the smallest part of it for hours.

We were attracted by their patience and their ability to make the best of even very trying conditions. One of the first things we learned to love about their often modest homes was the *tokonoma* (place of beauty). Even the most sparsely furnished home had one, that little crevice built into the wall and set aside for something of beauty—one lone blossom, one plum branch, a single vase saved from the ruin of their city—something, they would say, to feed their souls.

Still, it did not take us long to realize some of the longings, the lack of fulfillment, the confusion, and the spiritual hunger behind the smiling faces of so many of our new friends.

All of our lives we had known many wonderful people who did not know our God or the depth of his love expressed in Jesus Christ his Son. However, now, for the first time, we came face to face with the painful reality that there were millions of very religious, earnest, truth-seeking people in the world for whom the death of Christ for their salvation was, as yet, in vain.

Among the ninety-five million people in our new land we found fifty million Buddhists and over seventy million Shintoists, which meant that over twenty million of them were trying to be both at the same time. In all of my years in America I could not remember ever being surrounded by so many family altars as I was in our communities in Tokyo, Nagoya, and Yokohama.

Every morning I could see the wives around us rising very early to clean the altars, to put out freshly prepared rice as an offering to the ancestors enshrined there, and to burn fresh incense as an act of worship. I watched my

16

neighbors standing in the cold and the rain, clapping numb hands before a shrine, or ringing a bell before a temple, trying to arouse the attention of a god of stone. I listened as dozens of chanting young boys came to our gate carrying a heavy neighborhood shrine on their shoulders saying, "The god wanted to get out and walk among the people." I watched worried young mothers hurrying down the alley to tie the bibs of their sick children on little stone *Jizo* gods, hoping to find healing. I watched very old, weary travelers putting forth a last supreme effort to climb sacred mountains.

How often I whispered the words of Paul, "I bear them witness that they have a zeal for God, but it is not enlightened" (Rom. 10:2, RSV). Or again, I would echo the words of the psalmist. "Their idols are . . . the work of men's hands. Eyes have they, but they see not: They have ears, but they hear not" (Ps. 115:4-6, KJV).

From the very beginning we ran into people, many of them Americans, who said to us, "Why don't you leave these people alone? Can't you see they have a religion of their own?"

At first we could only answer that we had given ourselves to a God who said, unmistakably, "I am the way, the truth, and the life: no man cometh unto the Father, but by me" (John 14:6, KJV). In our hearts we would try to imagine what it would be like to face the troubles and problems, the decisions, the fears, the pain of this life without Christ to comfort and guide.

We had not been in Japan very long, however, until the people around us began to share some of these needs and to verify to us beyond any doubt that we had come to share a God of love they had never known, but desired very deeply.

17

2.
A First Look at the Longing

I will never forget her face. When Sumiko San finally got the courage to come across the alley to our mission compound, she had the look of a frightened, trapped animal. She spoke no English, and she had great difficulty in getting out even a few words of Japanese. We had seen her slipping quietly in and out of the small, seemingly very crowded house across the alley. We had heard from some of the other young people that Sumiko San was "different" and perhaps a bit unstable and confused.

In our still very limited Japanese we tried to show love and concern for her. Sometimes she just came and sat, saying very little; but she seemed to want to be there. Later we found small jobs for her so that she could earn a little money, which she seemed to need badly.

Little by little we were able to piece together the story. The memories in her young mind were just one great confusion of terror. She had been eight years old when the war had ended. This meant she had never known a time when her country was not at war. The last years of the war had meant constant bombings, fires, hiding in shelters, and the loss of her home and all the members of her family except her mother. One year before we arrived in Tokyo her mother had died, but there had been no

18

relatives, no money to bury her. The neighborhood people had taken up enough money to have her body cremated and the ashes placed in an urn. They had given this urn to Sumiko San, and she had been sleeping with it every night since.

We asked her about her living arrangements and were appalled by her answer. There were nineteen people living in that small house across the alley, and very few of them were related. They were just people like Sumiko San who had no other place to go. Each of them had a small bedroll made up of two Japanese *futon,* thick quilts, which they spread out in a small allotted place each night, but in which they had to roll up all of their possessions for storing during the day. It was here that Sumiko San kept the urn with her mother's ashes.

We tried, slowly and gently, to suggest that we would try to help get the money for burial; but her first reaction was—quite naturally, I suppose—"But she is all I've got!"

A long, careful process ensued before we could begin to get her to understand that there is a God and heavenly Father who loves and cares for his children. Only as she came to understand that was she finally willing to allow us to help arrange for the funeral and burial of her mother's ashes.

Some of the needs we met were less dramatic but just as deep and urgent. I remember especially the coming of Kato San.

It is unusual to meet an attractive, cultured Japanese woman the way I met Kato San. She dared to put aside the customs that would have made our introduction wait on a third party. She came to the door of my Tokyo home and introduced herself.

19

"I have a problem," she said, "which is troubling me greatly. I want so much to talk to you."

I invited her in. After leaving her Japanese *geta* in the entrance, accepting the slippers I offered, she sat with me in the living room while we went through the usual formalities of hot tea, cakes, and introductions. I found that she was the wife of an official in a large bank and that she lived in the nearby apartments for bankers' families. But she was obviously anxious to get back to her problem.

"It concerns my little six-year-old girl," she confided. "I have heard that you are a Christian missionary. I have seen you with your children and see that you have a lovely little daughter about the age of mine. That is why I thought you might be able to help me.

"You see, until this year I have had my little girl at home with me much of the time. I have tried hard to teach her as I ought to prepare her for life in this difficult world. But, Mrs. Hollaway, she started to school this year. She was assigned to a school some distance away. Every morning I get her ready and hold her hand as we walk out to the big, busy thoroughfare where she catches the public bus. You know how crowded the buses in Tokyo are. Several usually pass us by, already terribly full, before one will finally stop. Even then, they usually seem too crowded to make room for even one small first-grade child. I feel the little hand let go of mine as she pushes her way in. She is swallowed up by the crowd and is soon gone, across this big, big, wicked city—alone. Oh, Mrs. Hollaway, at that moment I am always overwhelmed with the thought, 'There ought to be somebody, somewhere in this great universe to whom mothers could pray at a time like this.'

20

"All day long I wait and wonder. At four o'clock in the afternoon I go back out to that big, busy street and wait for bus after bus, until the one bringing my little girl arrives. Once again she puts her hand in mine. Her little face turns up to me, and her eyes and her lips are filled with many questions—questions she has gleaned from her day in this, the largest city in the world. I want so much to help her, to guide her aright, but I lack wisdom. Once again my heart fills with longing. Isn't there someone, somewhere to whom mothers can go for wisdom?"

Then she turned an anguished face to me. "Oh, Mrs. Hollaway, do you know anyone, anywhere, to whom mothers can pray?"

I was glad to tell her about our loving, waiting Father. I was glad to show her the way to him through his Son. I was glad to enlist her in our Bible class for neighborhood women, which met in our living room each Thursday morning. However, I could not then, nor have I until this day, been able to get away from the thought of millions of other women in her land who did not live near a missionary or someone they could ask. How many of them, I wondered, were carrying in their hearts this same deep longing for someone to whom they could pray?

Such experiences brought me back constantly to the realization of the preciousness of the gift I had in Christ. That night I tried to put it into a prayer which I could pray over and over to be sure that I did not forget the meaning Kato San had brought to me:

Oh, God, I do not come to you
As often as I ought.
I struggle under heavy loads
That I know should be brought

And left here at your feet before
They waste one precious hour
Or make me walk as one who had
No source of strength and power.

And still, O God, I cannot dream
Of life without you here
To come to, bringing constant needs
Of sin and doubt and fear.
I would not dare to face one day
Without you walking near,
To love, and live your life through me,
And make your purpose clear.

But help me to remember, Lord,
That millions walk alone,
Not knowing where to find you, God,
Not ever to have known
Your love, your balm, your sacrifice
At such tremendous cost.
Do not allow me to forget
The anguish of the lost.

Oftentimes we were amazed to find how long and how diligently some of these people had been searching. Kawada Sensei (*Sensei* means teacher) helped us to realize this when we purchased land from him to build nine new houses for language students, who were soon to be joining us from America.

We had learned from neighbors that the land had been the site of a large private school that went from kindergarten through college. Kawada Sensei's father had been president of this large school. Kawada Sensei himself had been a rather high official in the ministry of education and was very active in the postwar UNESCO organization. When we asked him what his father would have thought about building a Christian compound on his land, Kawada Sensei told us his father's story.

"I think my father would have been exceedingly happy," he told us. "You see, he wanted very much to know God. He traveled completely around the world in search of him. He paid his own expenses and stopped in many lands, studying different concepts of God. Finally he came to the United States and studied the Christian Bible. He did not have anyone to explain it to him, but he thought that it must hold the real truth. So he bought many Bibles. But by the time he got back to Japan the war had begun, and it was very unpopular to have a Bible because everyone associated it with America, our enemy. Nevertheless, my father set up booths and stood here on this very land handing out Bibles. 'Read this!' he would say to everyone who passed by. 'I think it has the word of truth we are all seeking!' He died without ever having anyone to explain it to him, but I feel he would be happy to think it is finally being taught on his land."

Mr. Kawada and his wife became Christians, and we continued to know them and work with them for a number of years. But oftentimes, when God seemed very real in our services, he would weep for the man who had searched so earnestly for God.

In the midst of such need we always felt inadequate, especially in our early days there, when our language was so limited. However, I think it may well be true that the best things the foreign missionaries have going for them are their own senses of inadequacy. We had no choice but to lean on God. We were rarely tempted to run ahead of him. We followed where he led, and he used our faltering ways.

I remember so well the joy of memorizing our first hymn in Japanese. We knew few of the actual words, but we knew the meaning—for it was a translation of "The Old Rugged Cross." We went with some of our friends to a little mountain village one weekend when we had only been in Japan a few weeks. We got permission from the men at the railway station to run an extension cord out of the station to set up a loudspeaker and a light. One of our group had practiced reading the story of the cross out of the Japanese Bible, and Ernest and I sang our duet. A crowd gathered; and though most of them had never heard a hymn or the Bible before, they seemed strangely drawn and invited us back as often as we could come.

God opened the doors, and we simply walked through in faith that he would use even our stumbling ways. One good example of how he worked has to do with another suicide plan.

A young girl who had been coming to the services on Sunday evening stayed one night after the service to ask a favor of Ernest. She said she worked in an insurance company in the heart of the city of Tokyo, and she felt that some of her co-workers would like to have a chance to hear about God and the Bible. She thought they would be willing to give up their lunch hour for this if Ernest would be willing to come. Ernest hesitated, for he had only been studying the difficult language a few weeks. She said some of the people there spoke some English, and she thought they could arrange for an interpreter. She was not sure how many would attend, but she thought there would be at least half a dozen.

When Ernest arrived there at noon on the following

24

Tuesday, there were over fifty young people eagerly waiting for him. Some time later we found out the difference that day made in at least one young lady's life.

"I had almost committed suicide the night before," she said. "I had bought the sleeping pills and made all my arrangements, but then decided I would go back to the office for just one-half a day and put my desk in order. I spent all morning doing this and was ready to go home to die. I could see no reason at all for living. All of my family had died in the war, and I was completely alone. I came to Tokyo, trained for a job, and eventually went to work; but I had no one to love and no one to love me. I could not find any meaning, just bare existence. So I had decided to quit.

"But that was before I heard about Jesus," she continued. "Just as I was preparing to leave, some of the other office workers said that someone was coming during the lunch hour to talk about Christianity and the Bible. They invited me to go along. I didn't see that I had anything to lose. Besides, my empty room and the pills would still be there later.

"I didn't realize how much I had to gain," she recounted. "For the first time in my life I heard about a God who really loved me, who wanted to help me, and who would guide my life. It was a miracle. In those few moments everything changed. Suddenly I wanted very much to live."

She did continue to live, but there is more to the story than that. She gave to Christ the life he saved that day and began to find great meaning in his purposes for her. She became a specialist in the use of Braille and was a member of a team that put Christian literature into the hands of the thousands of blind people in Japan.

3.
Hard Questions to Answer

Coming to Christ in the deep commitment that his call to us and his sacrifice for us demand is never easy. In any life it raises serious, probing questions. But when one comes to Christ from a background of complete ignorance of Christ's teachings and from a culture in which no one around him understands his struggle, his questions are often compounded.

Many times our Japanese friends brought such questions to us. When we felt that the situation was difficult, we tried to give answers gently, though uncompromisingly. Many of those questions and their emotional impact will remain with us always.

One of these probing questions came from Nishina San. They all began for him the night of his conversion. He said that he had scarcely been able to believe his good fortune that night as he returned from the business trip in northern Japan. Everything seemed to be going his way. He had been accepted into his family's business and was doing remarkably well. He had been sent on this trip with the agreement that if he were successful in it, he would receive a promotion and thus would be able to marry the girl he had been promised from an excellent family. The trip had been very successful, and he was hurrying home to report the good news that night as he stood in front of the train station in Nagoya.

As he stood there he had a feeling that his joy was not as complete as it should have been. He was well aware that most of his friends would say there was little else he could ask for—success at such an early age, a good job, a good marriage. Still, something seemed to be missing in his life. He was uncertain just what it was.

At this moment our mission automobile appeared, with its loudspeakers blaring out a message over and over again as it continued to circle the large, busy station. The voice on the speaker was asking a question that seemed to speak right to Nishina's heart: "Are you lacking something in your life? Do you feel there ought to be a better answer to life's question than you have found?"

The voice invited the listeners to an auditorium not far away, where we were holding the first evangelistic services we had ever held in this city of over one million people. Nishina glanced at his watch. It was almost time for the services to begin. He felt strangely drawn to the meeting. Was it a coincidence, he asked himself, that the only two contacts he had ever had with this group called Christians should come on the same day? On the train, earlier in the day, something had caught his attention and left him wondering. The train had been very crowded, and he was glad that he had gotten to the station early and waited in the long line so that he was one of the fortunate ones who had been able to get a seat. In the seat just in front of him sat an American woman. She looked tired, and he wondered how long she had waited for her seat.

Just then he was very surprised to see her stand up and give her seat to a young Japanese woman with a child on her back. As she stood in the aisle, she held onto the strap just above Nishina's seat. In his curiosity he sat forming

27

the sentence in his head in English, wondering if he could make himself understood.

"Is it custom in America?" he asked at last. "Why do you give hard-to-get seat?"

He was surprised when she answered him in Japanese. "People do not always do it even in America. I am a Christian missionary, and Christians in any country try to serve other people."

He had wanted to ask more but was afraid his questions might sound stupid, for he knew nothing at all about Christianity. So he changed the subject. But now, here was another chance to find out more. He decided to delay his return home for an hour or two.

That service changed everything in Nishina San's life. He heard for the first time about Jesus Christ and his love and his sacrifice. He was overcome with a desire to follow this Christ and find new life in him. At the close of the service he joined a great number of people who went forward to express a desire to know more about this faith. He signed a card, met with the young Japanese pastor for a while, and then disappeared into the night.

Much later that same night, when most of the city was asleep, he came to the small apartment of the young pastor. He had a *furoshiki*, a Japanese silk scarf, in which were tied a few personal belongings. He had gone home after the service with the news of his conversion. His family made it very clear to him—either he would forget this nonsense about Jesus Christ, or he would be disowned. He would lose his job with the new promotion, his home, his family, and his bride. Sadly he gathered the few things together and left.

As he stood before the pastor, all his anguish was echoed in his voice as he asked, "How much does Jesus ask of his followers, Pastor; how much does he ask?"

We had all faced the question before. It comes up frequently in a pagan culture where following Jesus is often not accepted. The young pastor looked straight at Nishina San and gave him the only answer possible. "He asks everything, Nishina San. He asks everything."

And every time a young Christian came through the night with his little *furoshiki* and this same question, I asked myself over again whether or not I was willing to pay the price. I tried to put my thoughts into a poem to keep myself reminded. I called it "His Bargain."

There can be no half-love,
   no half-surrender
     at Calvary.
One look at the brave young Christ
   who suffered there reminds me
     the way is not easy.
He faced his cup of suffering
   and sacrifice,
     separation,
       sin and death,
   and he drank its bitter dregs
     to the very end.
Beside his cup my cup seems small indeed.
But he reminds me of its contents:
   death to self
   complete surrender
   no longer I
   but he in me.
And as he hands the cup to me
I hear him say,
"Drink . . . all of it."

Questions like Nishina San's often brought a sense of renewal in our own lives as we determined to offer ourselves anew and more completely to our Lord. We were constantly faced with the fact that many of our Japanese converts had to pay such a price to follow Christ, while the way for us, by comparison, seemed simple. Sometimes this cost was so bound up in their culture that it was hard for us to comprehend the total impact of the decisions they faced or the questions they brought.

This was true in the experience of our friends Bob and Helen Sherer, missionaries to Kobe, Japan, as they worked with Nomura San.

Standing on the stoop at their back door, the Sherers could see over the picket fence into the yard of the Imada family. It seemed to them that every time they looked in that direction they saw a seventeen-year-old girl with old wartime pants on, her long hair braided, working very hard. She seemed to be constantly dashing from one task to another. Since no one else there seemed to be working at such a frenzied pace, they wondered what her status in the house was.

When the girl, Hiroko Nomura, began attending their Bible class, Bob and Helen were gradually able to piece the story together.

Nomura San was converted in the first evangelistic service they held in Kobe. Dr. Duke McCall and Dr. W. A. Criswell were on a world mission tour, and Dr. McCall was preaching the night Nomura San, along with over three hundred others, decided to follow Jesus.

Later that night the missionaries, the evangelist, the interpreter, and the Japanese pastor were back at the missionaries' house discussing the service when Nomura

San came and said she must talk to someone. She said that she would have difficulty talking to a man and that she would like to explain her situation to Mrs. Sherer.

Helen was putting her two small girls to bed. This was her first such experience with the Japanese language, and she was frightened. She told me later, "Some people pray for the gift of tongues. This was the only time I ever prayed that; but boy, I prayed for the gift of *tongue* that night—the Japanese tongue!"

Nomura San poured out her story. She was a virtual slave in the Imada home. Before she was born her father had become deeply indebted to this family. They had taken him into their home as a son, but his subsequent dishonest and immoral life had made it impossible for them to fulfill the usual obligations of parents. When he had married Nomura San's mother, that old debt still bore down upon them; and they felt permanently disgraced until it could be settled.

Consequently, her mother had offered them her oldest daughter. Nomura San was to live in the Imada home as a servant without pay to fulfill this old debt.

After her profession of faith she was able to continue coming to Bob Sherer's Bible class for a short time. However, the Imadas, who were devout Zen Buddhists, soon realized that what they had assumed was a desire to learn English was much more and that Nomura San was very serious about Christianity. They forbade her to come again.

One day Helen was in her backyard and had a chance to talk to Nomura San briefly across the fence. She asked her if she were able to read the Gospel of John they had given her.

Nomura San beamed and pulled the already worn little

31

paperback gospel from her pocket.

"I am memorizing it," she said. "I've already learned it to here."

She turned past the eighth chapter.

"Why are you doing that?" Helen asked.

"Because I know they will take it from me before long, and I want to have it in here," she explained as she touched her hand to her heart.

Nomura San told Helen that the Imadas were complaining about the little forty-watt bulb in her room she used to read her Bible.

"You see," she said, "Mr. Imada works in Osaka and doesn't get home until very late. Each night I must put the children to bed and then wait up to serve him his supper, care for him, and clean up afterward. The only time I have to myself when I can study my Bible is between midnight and five A.M."

She told Helen that when many of the neighborhood young people passed by her house on their way to the Bible study, she became angry that she could never have the opportunity. She said she would whisper to herself, "I want to go. I want to go so badly the aching will not stop."

She said she was saying this one day by her kitchen window as she peeled vegetables and became so absorbed in the thought that she peeled her finger instead.

The Kobe church planned a baptismal service for new Christians on Christmas Day. On Christmas morning the Sherers were having their breakfast when Nomura San came bursting into the room with tears streaming down her face, saying, "Mrs. Imada is the meanest woman I have ever known!"

Then she told how much she wanted to be baptized.

32

She had asked her mistress whether, if she worked hard all day, she might be off for a couple of hours about four o'clock to go see her friends.

Instead of giving her an outright negative answer, Mrs. Imada had said, "Why, yes, it is Christmas Day, and I think you can be off for a little while *if . . .*"

Then she had proceeded to give her an impossible list of things that she must do before that time. She must clean the house, clean the storehouse out back (several days of work in itself, as that had not been done for some time), clean the yard, and so on.

"I couldn't possibly get it all done in three days, much less by four this afternoon. I want so much to be baptized."

The pastor was there and counseled with her, telling her that she was a Christian and pleasing to the Lord, whether or not she was able to arrange for the baptism. But when she had gone back to her work the pastor said he wished they could arrange a baptism for her, even if they had to smuggle her out late at night for a special ceremony.

In the end that is just what they did. She slipped over to the missionaries' house at ten-thirty that Christmas night; and the pastor, the missionary, and a few members went with her to be baptized.

"I can see her yet," Helen told me. "She had her long hair over that old kerosene stove of ours and was trying to get it dry and get back home in her bed before the Imadas knew what had happened."

She never was allowed to come to the church again. All the feeding she received as a new Christian were those occasional over-the-fence conversations and her personal study of the Bible. But she was faithful in that and in prayer, and she continued to grow.

The Sherers had been in touch with Duke McCall in America, keeping him posted on the progress of the church and its new converts. They told him of Nomura San's struggle; and he, in turn, told the story in a sermon in a church in Owensboro, Kentucky. A beautiful thing happened. A nineteen-year-old girl heard the story and was so touched by it that she wrote to the Sherers in Japan. She told them that she had not been able, for financial reasons, to go on to college with her friends who had graduated from high school; but she was working in a factory to save enough money to go later. She offered to withdraw all of her savings and send them to Japan if there was a chance that they might help purchase the freedom of this Japanese girl.

"You see, she is just my age," she wrote, "and I feel sure that nationalities make no difference in the hopes and dreams of a nineteen-year-old-girl."

Years later Bob Sherer had the privilege of meeting this girl in Alabama and was surprised to find her in a wheelchair. She had never mentioned her affliction when she offered to send all of her savings to help Nomura San.

No money ever actually changed hands, for Nomura San became convinced that her years of hard work had more than paid the debt. She wanted to free herself so that she could serve her new master, Jesus Christ. She went to the Imadas and told them this and said that she was leaving. Mrs. Imada became very angry and went to the Sherer home and angrily blamed them for all that had happened. Nevertheless, Nomura San did move out; and Bob and Helen were able to find her a job in a mission-

34

ary's home until she got on her feet. She subsequently joined another missionary, Annie Hoover, in Hokkaido; and they have worked together as a most remarkable team in all the years since that day. She has become an outstanding interpreter, has learned to play the organ, helps in the Hokkaido radio ministry, made a trip to America, and audited classes she needed at one of our seminaries.

But once a year Nomura San faithfully returns to her original family, the ones who gave her away. She says that every time she goes, they call the family together and sit around on the floor in a big circle and tell her what a failure she is. They remind her that she has been a Christian all these years and has neither made a marriage nor accumulated any money. In their eyes she is a complete failure.

So the question that Nomura San poses is one that so many of our Japanese young people must ask in the face of all the criticism they receive for their faith: "What is a failure?"

Not long ago Helen Sherer made a trip to Hokkaido and was able to talk to Nomura San. Nomura San told Helen of her joy in her work, of offers of advancement she had turned down to remain in the ministry she loves and does so well. Helen told her she would like to ask her one question: "Nomura San, do you still read your Bible the way you did in those early days?"

Big tears welled up in her eyes as she answered, "Sensei, if I couldn't have time every morning and every evening to read my Bible and talk with my Lord, I would be nothing."

And in her heart Helen echoed, "But with it you are everything. Who can dare to label your life a failure?"

The world may cry out, "You are nothing!
Your life is all failure and loss.
You had such great possibilities
Till you left them all at the cross."

We know his gospel is foolishness
To a world that does not believe.
But in our own hearts is the glory
Of the new free life we receive.

For we know that all else is nothing.
Without him we'd be nothing, too.
But in him we have the assurance
Of life so abundant and true.

We can only pray for those poor ones
Who know not and can't understand:
Only with him we are everything,
As long as we walk hand in hand.

A similar situation, yet one fraught with more futility and loss of meaning, came the day that Hirano San lost his son. He came to us with the burning question, "I have tried so hard, for so long. Was it all in vain?"

It had a great impact on my life, especially because of what had just happened in our home to our own sons the week preceding the accident.

For over ten years we had dreaded that week. From the time we had brought our sons to Japan with us when they were five and six years old, we had been conscious of the approach of the day when we would have to send them back to America to study and begin a new life. Unless something unforeseen happened, we knew that they would never return to the home they had loved so much in Japan.

They were sixteen and seventeen that day we took them to Yokohama to board the huge ocean liner alone. We stayed on board with them until the last signal was given for visitors to go ashore. Then we went down to the dock to catch the gay streamers they threw down to us from the deck above. We held onto the streamers as long as we could as the ship pulled away from the dock. We stood waving until they were too far out in the harbor to distinguish figures. Then, without speaking or planning, we drove our car up to the highest bluff overlooking the harbor to wave some more. As if by prearrangement, our boys climbed up as high as they could on the ship and were waving to us.

When they disappeared into the oncoming night, we drove back to Tokyo and the feel of our empty house. We had three younger children at home, aged four, five, and seven, so we tried to keep up a happy front. But our hearts were pure gloom.

On the following Sunday disaster came to Hirano San. Ernest had to be out of town on mission business that day, and I had gone alone to the little mission we were helping to start in a nearby kindergarten. During the service that morning two policemen came to the door and called Hirano San out of the meeting. After they had given him a piece of paper, the three of them left together. I was disturbed by the look on Hirano's face. It was almost time for me to play for the closing music of the service, so I waited. As soon as the service was over, another one of our members and I hurried to the nearby police station to try to find out what had happened. We soon learned that the piece of paper the policemen had brought Hirano San had been a telegram, which had read something like this: "Please come to Yokohama at once and claim the body of your son, who was drowned in the bay this morning."

Several of us stayed and waited together to be there when he returned. As we waited, I thought about Hirano San and the long struggle he had had. Several years before, during the war, he had felt a great hunger for God but had not known where to go for leadership. He had bought a Bible and had begun to study on his own. He was a very unlearned man, steeped in the traditions of his country and of Buddhism. For seven long years he had studied alone with no one to explain to him any of what he read. By the time he had come to us he was so confused and had so many questions and misconceptions in his mind that he had had nearly two years of counseling and guidance before he was ready to follow Christ in baptism. Now, as a young Christian, he had looked forward to leading his family to Christ. The boy the telegram had referred to was his oldest son, who was just finishing high school and had gone to Yokohama on his senior outing.

It was late in the afternoon when Hirano returned. None of us was prepared for what we saw as he entered the gate. He was carrying the body of his dead son in his arms. He had been so crushed and grief-stricken at the sight of his boy that he had insisted on boarding the train back to Tokyo with him in his arms.

Tears were streaming down his anguished face as he cried out to us, "I had just come to understand enough to try to bring him to Christ. Now it is forever too late. I tried so hard. Was it all in vain?"

I went home that night very ashamed—ashamed of a grief that had taken too little into account. It seemed now a self-centered grief that was out of perspective. What if my sons should never come home again under the roof of the home we had known together? It was, after all, a temporal home—one of small significance as compared to the one we would share together near the throne of God. How my heart ached for Hirano San and the anguish he felt. I could see in his face the cry of Lamentations 1:12, "Is it nothing to you, all ye that pass by? behold, and see if there be any sorrow like unto my sorrow" (KJV). I reminded myself over and over, "No matter what this little life span brings of grief and separation, it is but a moment compared to the eons to be shared in that house not made with hands, eternal in the heavens. My sons will be home!"

As we tried to comfort Hirano San we reminded him of the fine younger son still left in his home and of his wife who had no Savior to comfort her. It was not too late for them. Nor was it too late for his many, many friends, and ours, who were trying to face difficult situations without a Comforter or a Guide.

Later, when I was alone, I wrote down this reminder to myself so that I, too, would always remember the answer we were trying to give Hirano San.

Don't Let Me Forget

With every day I live, Lord,
   I am grateful that I know you.
I wonder over and over again
   how I could make it without you . . .

> but don't let me get
>> so peaceful in your presence
>> so confident in your power
>> so caught up in your love
> that I forget there are men . . .
>> millions of men
> who have to make it without you
>> every day
>> all the way.

They have never met you, Lord.
No one has offered them an introduction.

But the hardest question for me to answer was the one Mori San asked. It was not so difficult because we didn't *know* the answer. It was difficult *because* of the answer.

We met Mori San during our first two years in Japan while we were studying the language. He was a fine, intelligent young contractor who was helping to build mission houses. Ernest was responsible to the mission for the nine language houses being built on the language school compound at that time, so Mori San was in and out of our house a lot.

Besides this, his very attractive younger sister, Yoshiko San, had lived with us and helped in our home for many months. Yoshiko San had become a radiant Christian, and we longed to win Mori San; but he seemed to have many reservations.

The encounter with him that still stands out vividly in my mind occurred during the time when we were trying to decide where we would go to open evangelistic work when we completed our language study.

One night in our living room, Mori San asked us where we thought we would be going. We told him we thought we would be moving to Nagoya, Japan's third largest city. Nagoya had over a million people, but it was the center of a prefecture that had over three million people. Our Japanese pastors had been careful to point out to us that it was the center of an industrial area of over seven million people. As yet we did not have one single church in that entire area. In many parts of the area no Christian group at all had any witness.

Mori San looked disappointed. "When do you think my hometown will ever get a missionary?" he asked.

"How big is your town, Mori San?" we queried.

He hung his head.

"That is the trouble," he replied. "It's just a little mountain village. It is just a little old town of twenty thousand people."

Sorrowfully, we had to agree with him.

"Yes, Mori San, we are sorry; but at the rate our churches are supporting missions at the present, we cannot see even out there on the dim horizon a time when towns of twenty thousand can have a full-time Christian witness, missionary or Japanese. We can send Bibles. We might plan a few weekend evangelistic tours. But full time . . . not for many years."

We tried to explain it to him. "Mori San, we do not have a single witness in a town of under two hundred thousand. In fact, we have dozens of towns that large, two hundred thousand or more, that are waiting for their first witness."

"But let me tell you about my town," he insisted. "No one in my whole town had ever seen a Bible or heard about Jesus until twenty-five years ago, when a young Christian schoolteacher was assigned to a job in our town. He brought his Bible with him. When he found out

41

there was no church in the town, he called the people together to hear the Bible. He wasn't a preacher or anything. He just read the Bible to them once a week. He was just there one term before he was transferred somewhere else. But when he left he gave them his Bible.

"That was twenty-five years ago, Sensei, but the people in that town are still reading that Bible and praying for someone to come to live there who can explain it to them. For a long time they met every week.

"During the war, our town was heavily bombed because the Americans knew we had a munitions factory there. The people hid in caves in the side of the mountains to escape the bombs. I have seen them kneel in those caves and pray, 'God of the Bible: Those men up there in the planes, they live in a land where everyone has a chance to know you. Some of them must know you, God. Won't you end this war and send them home with their bombs and send them back with their Bibles?'

"Can't you see," Mori San asked quietly, "why I have a hard time believing that you Christians believe what you teach when you give me an answer like that to the question 'When will my town have a missionary?' "

4.
A Taste of Victory

Many days I awaken with the desire to sing, "God is so good. God is so good." I am constantly overcome with his generosity, his nearness, his willingness to forgive, his abiding love, and, especially, the fact that he chooses to entrust "this treasure in earthen vessels" and reach out to men in need with his mysterious drawing power through frail, imperfect human beings.

It was ever so in Japan. I do not mean to leave the slightest impression through my stories thus far that everything was discouraging, difficult, or overwhelming. There was that element, but God was at work; and there was tremendous joy in just watching his power at work. Many of the victories we watched him win in human lives remain in our hearts today to encourage us that we are never left to do his tasks with only our own feeble efforts.

Paul's observation in 2 Corinthians 12:10, "When I am weak, then am I strong" (RSV), has been the experience of us all. So often in the midst of our greatest discouragement he steps in with his power. This was true of the mission that was meeting in our home in Tokyo. Dr. Theron Ferris was a language student on the adjoining compound at the time and served as pastor of our little group. I was pianist, hostess, and general flunky.

We were in a period when we had gone some time without any conversions. In postwar Tokyo there was a great surge of interest in learning the English language. I suppose that it was natural that we attracted a fairly large number of rather cocky, cynical university students. They usually came with a rather thinly veiled purpose of practicing and learning conversational English.

We had discussed this situation after a Wednesday night prayer service. We decided that we could do very little about it and would just have to turn the problem over to the Lord, hoping that he would "work things together for good."

On the following Sunday evening we were a little discouraged when our next new participant expressed himself very openly on the subject.

"I want you to know from the beginning," he said, "that I have no interest in Christianity. My father is the president of a large department store chain, and he is very anxious for me to learn English. I am willing to listen to your talk about Christianity if you will help me with my English."

It was a bargain we had made many times. We had to admit that his honesty was refreshing. We each offered a silent prayer committing the service and this new student to the Lord.

We could see that some change was taking place as we watched his face during the service. We could feel the presence of the Holy Spirit, and we could only pray that the students could feel it too.

However, even we were a little startled by what happened. Only three Sunday nights later this young man came before the group to profess his faith in Christ. I shall never forget his statement.

"I thought that God, if he existed at all, was something high up and far away," he said, "with very little connection to my present life and all of the problems I face every day. That was my feeling until three weeks ago."

His voice softened and his eyes filled with tears as he continued.

"I had never taken into account a God who, three minutes after I came into a room where people were worshiping him, would be standing right beside my chair!"

I went to my room that night, and in humble gratitude I wrote this poem:

Empowered

O, Holy Spirit, this I know:
I cannot walk alone.
The words I speak seem hollow,
Men's hearts as cold as stone.
The work of faith that I would do,
Though good intent is there,
Comes bounding back, a hopeless farce,
And leaves me in despair.
But when you come into my soul
And fill it with your power,
When you possess this heart of mine
And walk with me each hour,
Then all of life has meaning deep
And in each passing day,
I know the joy of victory
For God . . . through hands of clay.

Another lesson I learned more clearly through one of our young converts was that of the power of God to deal with guilt in our lives.

Iwai San had been trained from his childhood to do one thing: to be a loyal, unquestioning, self-sacrificing soldier for the emperor. As he told us his story he said, "During my thirty-five years I have killed many times. I had been taught to do it as a patriotic duty and to feel very little personal involvement or guilt.

"But that was before the day on an island in the Pacific when it all became very real to me. I was ordered, along with four other soldiers, to take a group of prisoners out and have them dig their own graves. We did not have enough supplies left to feed them, we were told; and unless we destroyed them we might all die from starvation.

"When they finished digging the long trench that was to be their grave, we were ordered to kill them. They began to plead for their lives. They could not speak Japanese, but they took pictures out of their wallets. They showed us pictures of mothers and wives and children who were waiting for them. They made the sign of prayer with their hands and seemed to be trying to show us that people were praying for them. They bowed themselves completely to the ground in front of us in a desperate plea. But we were ordered to shoot them all.

"That night, back in my jungle tent, the long siege of guilt began. I could hear their pleading. I could see the people in the pictures. I imagined I could hear them praying and crying.

"In the days ahead I tried to hide my guilt in more blood and new heroics for the emperor. It did not help.

"Finally the war came to an end, and I went home to

Yokohama. The joy of all the things I had waited so long for was destroyed by my guilt.

"When my mother came to greet me and cover me with tears of joy, I saw the faces of the mothers in the pictures. When I married the girl who had waited out the war years for me, I saw the face of a young bride in one of the pictures. Most unbearable of all was the birth of our son. They brought him to me, and I wept as I saw the faces of the children whose fathers I had buried.

"I thought that I would lose my mind. I went to temples and shrines. I went to priests and bathed in sacred rivers, seeking purification. Nothing would absolve the guilt.

"Then, at last, one day I went to a Christian meeting and met Jesus Christ. He stooped down to where I was, in my sin and my guilt. He stoops to the lowest, the most unworthy, and forgives and loves and washes clean. It is a miracle. Only a great God could heal so great a guilt!" he cried.

The sheer joy and triumph of his testimony sent me away singing:

What can wash away my sin?
Nothing but the blood of Jesus;
What can make me whole again?
Nothing but the blood of Jesus.
Oh! precious is the flow
That makes me white as snow;
No other fount I know,
Nothing but the blood of Jesus.

I found another victorious answer in the aftermath of the war in the story of a young tailor in Hiroshima. He came out of the war simply devoured by hate. It took him a long time to see that, true to its nature, it was about to destroy him. Those who knew his story could well understand his feelings, but were sorry to see what those feelings were doing to him.

He and his sister had worked together in a shop in Hiroshima before the atom bomb had been dropped. On that fateful August day he had traveled to a neighboring city to make some deliveries and pick up some materials. He was on his way home but was still many miles from the city when he saw the blinding light and heard the impact in Hiroshima.

Although he had little knowledge as to what had happened, he hurried toward the burning city. He could not believe the destruction and terror that lay before him. It took him three days and nights to make his way across the city to the section where his shop had been. Everywhere about him was the debris of his city, filled with the misery of the dead and the dying.

When he finally came to what he surmised to be his section of the city, he could not find either his home or his shop. He ran frantically from one torn body to another, looking for his sister.

Finally, from a little mound of almost unrecognizable flesh on the ground before him, he heard the whisper of his name. There were no clothes left on the flesh, but he saw with horror that the print of the dress his sister had been wearing when he saw her last was burned into the heap of agony before him.

He called her name and knelt down beside his dying sister. She was trying very hard to say something to him.

"I hate them. I hate them," she whispered with great effort. "I hate the Americans."

48

Then she was gone. With all his heart the young tailor resolved, "As long as I live I will hate them, too."

When enough of the debris was cleared away from the city for a few scattered businesses to begin work again, the tailor secured a job in a small tailor shop that was trying to help the remaining citizens piece back together enough fabrics to clothe themselves.

All of his life seemed to have lost its meaning. He cared for nothing. He even took poor care of himself. He was simply consumed by his passionate hate.

A young Christian, the son of a deacon in one of the churches of the city, worked next to him in the tailor shop. The lad tried to make friends with the tailor and bring him out of his prison of hate.

"There is only a part of three outer walls of our church still standing," he told him. "We have been able to find only eleven members remaining of our congregation. But our pastor is still alive, and we meet in the shadow of those crumbling walls and sing praises together. It does us good. I wish you would come along."

"Isn't it a Christian church?" asked the tailor.

The boy nodded.

"Aren't the Americans Christians?"

"Many of them are," he agreed.

"Then I will never, never have anything to do with it," the tailor declared.

Weeks and months went by, and the deacon's son went about reconstructing his life and his church.

The tailor continued in his bitterness and hate until he felt completely desperate.

Finally he asked the lad, "What am I going to do? Life is not worth living at all."

The boy tried again. "I wish you would come with me

49

tonight and just listen to the music. You could leave before the message."

"Well . . . just the music," the tailor finally agreed.

That night he felt a strange warmth within his breast as he met with the little group and listened to them sing. Although he left as soon as the music was finished, he came back again many times. Finally, one night, he felt so intensely moved he felt he had to stay to hear the message.

Christ spoke to him during that service. He told him of his Father, who was waiting with open arms to receive him, love him, heal him.

At the close of the service he could only rush forward crying, "I want him for my Father!"

"He wants to be the Father of us all," the pastor quietly reassured him.

The tailor suddenly stopped and grew very still, remembering. Finally he asked, trembling, "Is he the Father of the Americans, too?"

"Of many of the Americans, yes," the pastor replied.

The struggle going on inside him was evident on the tailor's face as he stood there. Finally the struggle ended. A great smile broke across his face.

"If we have the same Father, then we must be brothers!" he cried joyfully.

It has helped me through the years to remember that my Father can heal even hatred as intense as that. Surely he can teach me the meaning of brotherhood. I tried to put it into words in this poem published in *A Field of Diamonds* (Nashville: Broadman Press, 1976).

   His Child?

I find no concept quite so hard to grasp

50

And yet so full of comfort, joy, and love
As this . . . that the Eternal Lord, our God
Should welcome me before his throne above
And let me call him Father, as a child,
Beloved, forgiven, nurtured as his own,
Reminding me that the blood his Son has shed
Has bought for me a place before his throne.
But yet another truth stands parallel:
I have no right to call him Father still,
Unless I can accept the simple fact
That every single creature in his will
Is his child, too . . . loved as any other,
Each one, my Father's child . . . each, my brother.

A case of victory that I had no personal part in but that was witnessed by several of our seminary students in Fukuoka, Japan, has meant a lot to me. It seems a symbol of the victory Christ brings as his children face death and eternity.

It took place in a hospital on an island in southern Japan. It is a place where there is often very little hope or happiness. It is an isolation hospital for hopeless tubercular patients. When this group of seminary students decided to make regular trips to the hospital, they little dreamed how Suzuki San would bless their own lives. They knew only that few of the patients had ever heard of Jesus Christ or his gospel of love. They hoped to take him to these patients through singing, Bible reading, and personal testimonies.

On their first trip, however, they came to the door of Suzuki San's room. She had heard their singing down the hall and realized that at last her prayers had been answered and some Christians had come to witness in this hopeless place. When they came to her door, she smiled and waved them on as she called out joyfully, "God be praised! Do not waste your precious time on me. You see, I already know the blessed Savior. Look!"

She pointed a thin, frail finger to the words she had written on the hospital wall above her bed. The entire twenty-third psalm had been laboriously scrawled there.

"The Lord *is* my shepherd," she cried triumphantly. "Please go and share him with the others."

Each time the little Christian group came it was the same. Suzuki San was overjoyed to see them but always waved them on to the other patients.

Then the day came when she appeared to be waiting for them. She beckoned them into her room.

"Today I want you to sing just one song for me," she told them quietly.

She pointed a bony finger up to the wall and, trembling, underlined the words, "Though I walk through the valley of the shadow of death I will fear no evil, for thou art with me."

"He is so precious," she whispered.

The little group sang the song she requested. It was "Nearer, My God, to Thee." In just a short while Suzuki San quietly and peacefully closed her eyes and followed her shepherd home.

It seemed as if a benediction had passed over the little group that would linger for the rest of their lives.

I have tried to capture the victorious spirit of Suzuki San in this poem:

My Shepherd

Though I walk through the shadow I fear not,

For my shepherd is walking with me,
And he knows every step of my pathway.
Oh, the comfort to know he can see
Beyond the blind curve of tomorrow
To that land of unending day;
And the journey will be, oh, so joyful,
With my shepherd to show me the way.

Suzuki San left behind her only two requests. The first was that she should have a Christian funeral. The second was that her grave be marked with a simple cross with only two dates upon it—"The only two dates in my life of real importance," she said. "The date I came to know the Lord and the date I went to live with him in paradise." It seemed so fitting that a young boy made a profession of faith at her funeral.

5.
Sunshine and Shadows

As I finished portions of this manuscript and asked numerous friends to read it, one frequent comment was, "It is pretty heavy. Did you feel that way all of the time?"

My answer was, "In a land where 99 percent of the people are dying without any knowledge of our Lord, you never get very far from that fact."

However, we weren't in Japan too long before the Mission Board's dream of at least one hundred missionaries became a reality. This missionary fellowship kept us all going. Of course we shared our sorrows, our tasks, our dreams. But one thing that helped all of us was sharing our laughter. Every time we had a chance to get together I was reminded of the line from Proverbs, "A merry heart doeth good like a medicine" (Prov. 17:22, KJV), for we all came away feeling better.

Any time many Americans burst in upon another culture, with all of the adjustments, the slow acquisition of the language, and the differences in culture, a lot of humorous things are certain to happen. We enjoyed sharing many of these occurrences with each other.

In postwar Japan labor was very cheap and people everywhere were looking for work, so most of us had help in our homes to free us for more mission work and language study. Most of these people knew no English at all, and we were just beginning to study Japanese; so communication left a lot to be desired.

One of my favorite stories is of the maid who was going to make her first American biscuits. The missionary wife explained about mixing the flour and salt and leavening, the careful working in of the shortening, and, finally, the addition of the milk. The Japanese girl repeated it all, wrote it down, and seemed to understand. She promised to come in a little early the next morning and cook biscuits for breakfast.

As soon as the missionary wife heard her in the kitchen that morning, she got up and quickly dressed to go in and supervise the task. However, she wasn't prepared for what she saw when she entered the kitchen. The Japanese girl had mixed all of the other ingredients on a small counter top. Now she had just added the milk and was running around the table, frantically brushing up the milk with rapid hands, trying to keep the milk from running off the table. It had not occurred to the missionary until that very moment to tell the girl to mix the dough in a bowl!

We learned by a similar experience that we should not ever assume any knowledge of our way of life, but should be very explicit in all of our instructions. It was long before the day of the modern refrigerators with icemakers, but we had taken an electric refrigerator with us. Few Japanese had ever seen one in a home before. One of the first nights we attempted to entertain guests for dinner, we warned our Japanese helper that we would get home from language school too late to make more ice. If she used the ice during the day, she would need to be sure and make some more. She agreed. But just as we were almost ready to sit down to dinner that night, I went to get the ice and found only empty trays.

"But I asked you to make the ice!" I remonstrated.

"*Me* make ice?" she asked in an amazed tone. "You told me this machine would make ice. I put in the trays and waited."

Our guests probably enjoyed the memory of her innocent protests much longer than they would have remembered the cool drink, anyway.

Some of the embarrassing times we had trying to learn the difficult language were eased somewhat by being able to laugh about them later with our friends. Many words were made entirely different by one vowel sound. One of our missionary friends was invited to a formal Japanese wedding. After the ceremony everyone was saying a word to the bride and groom. He thought he knew a good sentence to say, so he walked up and said enthusiastically, *"Kireina kemono, desu ne!"* He was surprised at the look this brought to many faces. He was confused because he thought he had said, "What a beautiful kimono!" But later some of his Japanese friends explained that what he actually had said as he looked at the blushing bride was, "What a beautiful beast!"

One of our missionary wives was upset because a contractor who had built a number of missionary houses seemed to be using an inferior grade of plaster. Great cracks were later appearing in many of the ceilings. The word for crack in Japanese is *hibi,* but when Helen tried to describe the problem she got mixed up and said *hebi,* which means snake. Imagine the consternation of the poor contractor when she told him, "Something must be wrong with your plaster. All of the mission houses you plaster look all right at first, but in a few weeks great snakes come out of the ceilings!"

Of course, many of the Japanese who tried to learn English by listening to a lot of us Southerners had a good bit of trouble also. I remember the day that attractive, intelligent Yoshiko San came up to us with a question. "Would you please tell me what one English word means? You say it all the time and I have looked in every dictionary, but I cannot find it. It is the word 'whatdjasay?'"

One of our best Japanese interpreters was a professor at the famed Tokyo University. It was arranged for him to have a study trip to America, and he phoned Ernest for an interview, saying he had two important questions to ask him pertaining to the trip. We were not too surprised when he arrived and we found the first question to be, "How do you take a bath in America?"

In a Japanese bath you wash yourself completely *before* you get in the tub. You dip hot water from the tub and wash off all soap before getting into the clean tub of water to soak and relax. He had seen American movies in which people seemed to be washing *in* the tub, and that was very hard for him to imagine. However, it was a question we were glad he asked. We had had Japanese to visit in American homes who had not thought to ask that question before trying to take a Japanese-style bath in a bathroom that had no drain in the floor to carry off the excess water. You can imagine the water that came running out under the door!

But his other question took us by surprise. It was "Please, would you teach me how to kiss?" At that time kissing in public was never done in Japan even by husbands and wives, but this man had seen enough American movies that he assumed he could never spend a few months in the States without being expected to follow this seemingly much-used custom. He must have managed all right because he met and became engaged to the daughter of the publisher of the *Japan Times,* the largest English newspaper in Japan.

Even after we had been in Japan long enough that we did not make so many mistakes in language and customs, we still had some embarrassing moments because of the social customs to which we could never quite become accustomed. One of these was the custom of sitting for hours on the *tatami* floor with our feet drawn up under our bodies. (Remember that shoes were removed and everyone was in stocking feet.) Ernest was at a meeting of the national secretaries of our various departments since he was national Sunday School secretary. On this particular day he was seated next to the lady who was the head of our national women's organization. The meeting was unusually long, and Ernest's feet had long since gone to sleep. He reached down to scratch them, trying to get a little feeling back into them, and was surprised that he couldn't even seem to feel the scratching. He wondered why the sedate lady at his right seemed so restless. Finally one of the Japanese leaders saw what was happening and could contain his mirth no longer. Ernest was scratching the stockinged foot of the distinguished lady!

But some things were hard to laugh off. When we couldn't laugh we were thankful we could still pray and trust the Lord to see us through the shadows as well as the sunshine. We had to lean heavily upon him, for example, when any of our number died. There are no mortuaries as we know them here because Japanese usually cremate their dead. Consequently, a body to be buried must, according to the law, be in the ground within twenty-four hours. This meant that the men had to make the wooden coffin, and the women had to sit up most of the night making the lining and preparing the corpse. They were hard experiences, but God was very real in them. I think, too, we all felt a little nearer to our Christian forefathers in those times, for this must have been an experience common to them all.

For our own family I think the hardest time came when we had to leave the church we had helped to organize and build in Nagoya. The church had just gone through a traumatic experience (explained elsewhere in this book), and we did not want to leave the people. Besides, I was seven and one-half months pregnant with Mark; Stephen was not yet two; and Ernest had not been feeling well. We told ourselves Ernest was just tired from all the extra work at the church and all of the packing for furlough. However, before the ship was well out to sea he collapsed in our stateroom and did not take another step for several weeks. The ship doctor did not know what was causing the high fever and the loss of the use of his legs, but he suspected polio; so he isolated him for the trip.

The president of our seminary in California met the ship and bodily carried Ernest off. After taking us to his home, he later took us to a train for the trip to a hospital in Dallas. Ernest's illness was tentatively diagnosed as rheumatoid arthritis, but his fever finally left. He regained the use of his legs in time to get out of the hospital before I had to go into it to give birth to Mark. Before Mark was six weeks old our ten-year-old son, Bill, came down with polio and was paralyzed from his neck down.

I shall never forget that night. We were at my mother's home in Arkansas, preparing to leave early the next morning for North Carolina. My doctor brother was there and was suspicious that Bill's trouble might be polio. He did a spinal tap and was able to confirm it at the local hospital even before any of the dreaded paralysis set in. When the paralysis came he called some specialists in Dallas to confer with them and tell them how extensive it was. They told him there was very little chance that Bill would ever walk again. We thought Bill was asleep at that moment, but he heard my brother relay the message to us. In a moment I heard him calling me.

"I heard Uncle Bill," he said, but he did not seem greatly disturbed.

"When the little boy in the Middle East had polio, all the missionaries everywhere prayed for him—remember. Will they pray for me?" he wanted to know.

We assured him we would call the mission office in Richmond right away and get the prayer chain started.

A little later that night he saw our worried faces and asked, "Didn't you call them?"

"Yes," we told him. "We called."

"Then why are you still worried?" he chided.

He never seemed to doubt that he would be completely all right, and God rewarded his faith with a miracle.

It was a difficult fall. Ernest was hard at work on his doctorate; both of the younger boys required a lot of attention; and Bill had to be taught at home and given physical therapy every day while twelve-year-old Lee went to school. However, by January, Bill was able to be taken to school each day. By May he was able to ride the bicycle he had saved five years to buy. God was so good. He saw us through it all and gave us the added bonus of a baby girl to take back to Japan that fall with her four older brothers.

6.
Heartbreaks Come Too

God never promised us we would always win. He told us to go out and sow the seeds of his love and his grace. But he warned us from the beginning that some of the seeds would fall on stony ground, by the wayside, or among the thorns. He warned us that some who heard would have no roots; some would be choked by the cares of this world; some would be overcome by Satan. Still, that is hard to accept, and even in memory we ache for those we could not win.

The first day I saw Iwata San I didn't think she looked like much of a prospect for anything. The two pieces of cheap clothing she wore scarcely covered enough of her body to be decent. She had slipped into an old pair of sandals for the occasion, but her stained, gnarled old feet were obviously accustomed to going barefoot. The few teeth she had left were stained with snuff. But one thing I had to say for her from the beginning was that she was persistent.

"I came to work for you," she insisted. "I live down there," she said as she pointed in the general direction of the valley below our hill.

"I can see your house from there," she continued. "I've been watching you build it. I figured you were going to need help when it was done. My niece said you are hiring.''

"We *were* hiring,'' I corrected. "We can't afford much, but we have many guests here and are not accustomed to the Japanese marketing every day and cooking Japanese foods. That's why we decided to hire one person to live in and help. We have already filled that position.''

"I heard about that,'' she replied simply. "But you need me, too.''

"How is that?'' I asked.

"One Japanese helper can only help with the cooking and dishes and this big house. You have a big yard and children—and more coming!'' She laughed as she unabashedly touched my pregnant abdomen.

I laughed at her total lack of inhibition, which was so completely different from most of the Japanese I had met. But I told her I was sorry we couldn't use her.

"You have many guests, and that means much laundry. You have much work here, and I like work. I like flowers and children, too,'' she said, smiling her broad, toothless smile.

"But we cannot afford it!'' I insisted.

"You can afford me,'' she replied. "I work six days a week for only four thousand yen a month.''

My mind did a quick calculation. At the exchange rate at that time that was just a little over eleven dollars a month or about two and a half dollars a week. I could scarcely believe my mental figures, for they said that was about forty-two cents a day or a little over eight cents an hour. I certainly did not feel I could do my own laundry and yard and tend to my children for that. Still, I hesitated. I had never had one helper in my home in America. Surely I could manage without two.

I told her that I was sorry, but I thought we could make out all right.

"Well, I'm already here. I may as well just help you today," she announced.

She was such a simple person, and her motives seemed so transparent. I doubt that she had figured out that if I kept her around for a day or two I would want her forever. But that is what happened.

There were many things she could not do. She never came to understand many of our appliances. She did not know how to receive guests. She never looked very presentable. I had to keep her out of my kitchen for the most part. Her way of cooking spread grease and batter far and wide. She was accustomed to a dirt floor in this area, so she paid little attention to things spilled. But she had never claimed any of these abilities. She had only said she liked to work and that she loved children and flowers. And she certainly proved those claims to be entirely true.

I never knew her age for sure, but she was near sixty. She had several older grandchildren, I knew. Her hands were gnarled, and her back was bent.

I worried about the hours she put in. She never wanted to leave until she had finished whatever she was doing, even though I knew she still had her husband's supper to prepare and her own work waiting for her at home. When she left each week on the night before her one day off she would say, "If you need me before I get back, just call me."

She tried to protect me from hard work or lifting heavy loads, although I was about thirty years her junior. "You don't want a crooked back," she would chide.

I couldn't buy bulbs or plants or flowers to set out but

she would have them done before I could get to them.

"You don't want your hands to get like mine," she would say.

We had three babies born in the first four years she worked for us. Each one of these probably spent more of their waking hours strapped to Iwata San's back than they did in their crib. I chided her and told her she would wear herself out and spoil the children.

"Children get lonely," she would reply simply.

One moment I still cherish is the day I found her with my Stephen, then nearly a year old, strapped to her back while she was weeding and spading the flower garden. The work alone was too hard for her without the weight of the child. I went out immediately to get Stephen, but she would have none of it.

"It's nothing. It's nothing," she said. "Besides, little boys love spring gardens."

Needless to say, I loved her. Outside of my own children, I don't believe I ever wanted so much to win someone to Christ. I wanted to see her worn-out body someday made straight and beautiful and strong before his throne. I wanted to see her simple loyalty given to one who was worthy of it. Tears come to my eyes even now as I write of it. I cried many, many tears as I went about my housework listening to George Beverly Shea's recording of the song "Beloved Enemy," about those loved ones who were not on the Lord's side and would not join us in heaven. Even yet, there are songs in our present day which I can scarcely bear to hear, such as "I Wish We'd All Been Ready."

Iwata San was patient and listened to me many, many times as I tried to explain my beliefs to her and to introduce her to Christ. She would listen attentively, but

64

she would always shake her head and at the end say, "It is too much for me to understand.

"It is too late for me," she said. "I wish you could have come many, many years ago when I was young and searching. I think I might have understood then. But I have grown old with longing. I have climbed so many sacred mountains. I have washed in so many sacred streams. I have made so many long trips to shrines and bowed before so many temples. Sometimes my heart still longs for something more, but it is too late. I can no longer learn another way."

Her answer was final. We had to move from Nagoya after five years, and all my prayers and all my tears had no avail. Sometimes yet, I feel that when I get to heaven one of the first things I will do is to look around and see if some miracle in her later years could possibly have reached my Iwata San.

I recognize the fact that part of what hurt so much in the experience with Iwata San was the feeling of hopelessness—that she was incapable of choosing any other way. But it hurts, too, when the choice is deliberate, though wrong, as it was in the case of Okura San.

We had known Okura San's wife first. She was a pleasant, rather intense woman in her early forties. When she became a Christian, her first and immediate concern was for her husband.

When she seemed unable to share her newfound faith with him she came to us for help. She felt that perhaps a man could reason with him better, so she asked Ernest to visit him and try to make some impact on his thinking.

Ernest went to call on him, and we had him as a guest in our home. He was an intelligent, nice-looking high school teacher. He was obviously interested in Christianity, but some things seemed to pose great barriers for him.

In the first place, he was afraid of ridicule. He told us frankly, "Not one of our faculty is a Christian. Most of them are Buddhists. I have heard some slanderous remarks from time to time about people around us who desert our native faith and accept a 'foreign religion.' I wouldn't want to face that—at least, not as long as I am in my present position."

But the other answer he gave seemed more important to him.

"I have thought about it a lot," he said slowly and with meaning. "I do not believe I could face the fact of it. You see, if I were to become a Christian, you would not have any place to bury me if I died. I would be rejected as an outcast."

This seems like strange reasoning in our culture, but it was very acceptable in his. In Japan, the two main religions are Shinto and Buddhist. Since the Shintoists consider the dead body unclean, they do not want to have much to do with burying the dead. Consequently, they worked out a sort of reciprocal agreement with the Buddhists. Regardless of the deceased's affiliations (and many Japanese try to be both Shintoists and Buddhists at the same time), the Shintoists do the marrying and the Buddhists do the burying. Thus, the Buddhists own nearly all of the cemeteries and will not allow a Christian to be buried there.

We knew the truth in what Okura San was saying. We thought of those Japanese churches where we had seen rows of urns, containing the cremated remains of their dead members awaiting some place of burial. A limited number of our cities had Christian burial plots, but our town of Nagoya was not one of them.

Ernest made several more trips to Okura San's home, but this last reason for rejecting Christianity seemed to remain foremost in his mind.

Some weeks later we missed his wife in our services for a Sunday or two. We thought perhaps she was out of town. But then the following Sunday she came in late and sat down in the rear of the building instead of coming to her usual seat. During the service we noticed she was crying softly.

At the close of the service we hurried back to her and tried to ask her as gently as possible what was the matter.

For a long moment she did not speak. Then finally she blurted out her terse, sorrowful message: "My husband died last Tuesday."

We were stunned.

"We are so sorry. Why didn't you call us?" we inquired gently.

She looked at the floor and fingered the *sambika* (hymnal) in her hand.

"I was embarrassed to tell you what I had to do," she told us at last.

"You see, I felt I had to give him a totally Buddhist funeral with burial in the plot he had chosen. I thought I had no other choice since it was so very important to him. You know, he paid the price of his eternal soul for that privilege."

It was hard to comfort her, for we knew that what she said was true. We could only remind her that many of us get our priorities mixed up, too. We who know Christ need to be sure that we remember what things are first.

It was a message for my own heart. Priority fixing is never simple. It was always a complex problem for me in Japan, living in a country where the lost and the dying were about us all of the time. Still, I knew that even in my frantic concern, sometimes I lost sight of what Christ wanted to give me in my own life with him. I faced this fact anew and wrote the following with renewed dedication:

His Offer

I came to bring abundant life to you,
Yet you struggle on each passing day
With life that is so circumscribed and small,
Bound by the things which come within your view,
When I had planned that faith would lead the way
To unknown vistas where great duties call.
Why do you chafe beneath a load of fear?
I offer faith, love, soundness of mind.
You have my promise: "I will strengthen thee."
Why don't you look beyond your little sphere
And see the glories there for you to find
Walking along my sunlit path with me?
I came to bring abundant life to you.
Accept it . . . that is all you need to do.

But perhaps the failure that has had the most long-lasting effect in my life was a story I told in my previous book, *When All the Bridges Are Down*. It is important to this story, however, and I would like to tell it here with a little more detail. It is the story of my neighbor, Sanno San.

Like those of most missionaries, our first two years in Japan were spent in intense language study. We lived on a small compound with other language students. Every day we went down to an old stone church that had been

68

converted into a language school for foreigners. The distance was about a half-hour or so through the miserable Tokyo traffic. When we got there we sat huddled in the unheated, undecorated rooms in our overcoats, scarves, and gloves, and tried to concentrate on the classes that were taught totally in Japanese for four uninterrupted hours. Then we were supposed to return to our small houses and put in two hours of study for each hour of class. Few of us were ever able to hold out for the whole eight hours, but we tried very hard. Our schoolage children rode a bus to an army compound to attend school. Our younger children attended a Japanese kindergarten. All of the usual duties of shopping and housekeeping took more time than usual because of the language barrier and our unfamiliarity with Tokyo, the marketing customs, and so forth. Since there was little time for anything else, it was a lonely, frustrating two years.

One of the brightest spots for us during this period of time was Sanno San and her garden. This seems strange as we look back upon it, for we never did have any lengthy conversations with her. We were never entertained in her home, nor she in ours. Still, we enjoyed so much having her as our first neighbor; and she had a lot to do with our first favorable impressions of Japan and her people.

She lived in a fairly small, typically Japanese house with sliding doors and windows that were generally opened during the day to reveal the simple tatami mat rooms inside. There was a stone wall around the yard, but it was not so tall that we could not peer over it and see the miracle of Sanno San's garden.

Most Americans would scarcely have labeled it a garden, for it was no larger than an average American living room. But in the dull setting of the drab early postwar Tokyo, it was the one spot we could always count on that would have something of beauty in it. From the first little crocus that peeped up through the snow in late winter until the last bit of blazing color of her chrysanthemums in late fall, Sanno San always managed to have something in bloom. But almost more than her flowers, we looked forward to her smile. Sanno San was petite and polite and pretty. She was rather shy, more so perhaps with Americans because she did not know a word of English. But day after day she managed to watch for us as we left for language school, and she would come out and bow and smile and wave us on our way.

We longed to share our Lord with her, but didn't have enough confidence in our limited language ability to go much beyond surface exchanges during those first days. We gave her a Bible, tried to let her know we cared, and hoped for another chance later on.

It looked for a while as if that chance were really coming. We had been assigned to Nagoya for five years. We loved it there and had a good work going. I had to admit to disappointment when we were reassigned to Tokyo so that Ernest might become the national co-secretary for our Sunday School department, working out of Tokyo. Perhaps the greatest consolation for me in the move was the fact that our mission assigned us a plot of land on the other side of Sanno San's home on which we could build our house. We would be neighbors again! *Now,* I thought, *perhaps we will have the opportunity to win her.*

But those first days of our return were very busy. We lived in Yokohama, where there was a vacant mission house, and commuted back and forth as we tried to oversee the building of our house. The Japanese were anxious for Ernest to get started in his new work, and he was gone much of the time. There were many contacts to reestablish, and he had to make the decision about whether we should try to establish a church in our home. In all the rush we did find time to visit Sanno San, only to find that, in the interim, her husband had become a devout Zen Buddhist. Our neighbors warned that we must move very slowly, or we would alienate them entirely.

However, before very long we heard that Sanno San was ill. We went to inquire and found that she had been placed in a tubercular sanitarium some distance from Tokyo. We began to realize that the small body we had called "petite" might actually have been classed as frail. Even then, we failed to grasp the gravity of the situation.

It was one of those days when the clouds and the smog of Tokyo descended, and it looked like twilight in the middle of the afternoon. As I stood by my kitchen window, which faced Sanno San's house, I suddenly became aware that our whole yard had been flooded with light.

As I looked toward Sanno San's house, I was amazed at what I saw. So many of the sliding doors and windows had been thrown open or removed that it was almost as if there were no exterior wall on our side of her house. In the exposed interior I could see a huge altar. On the top of the altar there seemed to be a large picture of a woman. On all of the tiers of the altar were hundreds of small candles, all lit by tiny electric light bulbs. I had never seen so much light in a Japanese home. Electricity was at a premium in postwar Tokyo. Most homes had a limited number of outlets and normally used them very sparingly. I knew that what I was seeing must represent a great expense, but I did not understand its full meaning.

I hurried over to another neighbor, Suzuki San, to try to find out what was happening. She was a close friend of Sanno San. Perhaps she would have some answers.

"Sanno San died last night," Suzuki San told me sadly.

"What is the meaning of all the lights?" I asked her. "How long will they burn them? Aren't they terribly expensive? Is there something we can do to help?"

"No, we have taken care of everything," she replied. "Many of us who loved Sanno San so much have put all of our money together to do this for her."

What she told me next will remain etched on my soul forever.

"You see," she explained, "the soul of our Sanno San does not know the way to heaven. We believe that during the twenty-four hours after her death her soul will come back to the places it has known and loved, seeking help. We have bought all of the lights we could afford to try to help her soul find its way to heaven tonight."

You can imagine that I did not sleep very well that night. I was very conscious of the glare of those lights. I was much more conscious of the destiny of the soul of Sanno San and the pathetic futility of the efforts of her neighbors to try to find the home of Eternal God with little man-made lights. One Scripture kept coming to my mind: "If therefore the light which is in thee be darkness, how great is that darkness" (Matt. 6:23, KJV). But most of all, I was kept awake by the thought of millions of Christian people going complacently on their way, giving little thought to their Lord's admonition. "Ye are the light of the world!" (Matt. 5:14, KJV).

7.
God Giveth the Increase

I think the hardest lesson for Christian workers anywhere in the world to learn is that God's work is just that: *God's* work. If we follow his leading, he gives us a work to do for him, and it remains *his* work. We aren't responsible for the results, for the future, or even for completely understanding all that is happening or is involved in any situation. Sometimes we are discouraged, disappointed, or even angered and demand to know why things happen or fail to happen. But God doesn't always honor our demand. He answers simply, "Obey me. I will take care of the rest."

This was particularly true for us in Japan. With so many differences of background and culture, we often failed to understand how God was working and, indeed, sometimes wondered if he were working at all. Looking back, we can see that some of our greatest victories seen in the perspective of eternity, were, from the human perspective, obvious failures at the moment.

We worked with two great Tokyo churches, both with outstanding Japanese pastors, during our language study years. In the second of these, Tokiwadai Church, Ernest was elated at all the prospects for service. We had been with the church from its beginning in Pastor Matsumura's home. Ernest had helped draw the plans for the church building when it was erected.

There were many things he would have enjoyed doing there, but the task that was assigned to him as his chief responsibility was a difficult and discouraging one. He was asked to teach a class of unruly university students. They were from the best universities in Japan, which screen their students very rigorously; so these were very intelligent fellows from good homes. However, they were cynical to the point of being disruptive. They seemingly came to the class with two purposes in mind: to practice their English and to make fun of religion. They giggled and laughed and asked mocking questions. They were especially abusive during prayer time. Not only did they make no pretense of entering into the spirit of prayer, but they laughed and took a "Who does he think he is talking to?" attitude.

Ernest would come home each Sunday tired and discouraged.

"It's hard to see how I could be accomplishing anything at all," he would say. But he kept studying and praying and trying.

Even yet, it seems almost incredible that three future Christian leaders came out of that class. Under all of the seeming failure God was at work.

One of the most handsome and intelligent of these dissenters was a lad named Okamura San. Both of us admired him greatly, with his flashing black eyes, his finely sculptured features, and his gift of repartee. But it was hard to believe he would ever give God a chance to use him.

We remembered all of this quite vividly sixteen years later when we were having to leave our work in Japan to return to the States. Among all our Japanese friends, we found our greatest consolation in the fact that we had the able and consecrated hands of Okamura Sensei in which to leave all of the results of years of labor in the national Sunday School movement.

After his conversion Okamura San went to work with Ernest in this struggling Sunday School work, then in its infancy. He began as a translator, then became a writer, later an editor, and, finally, the co-secretary with Ernest for the work across the nation. When we were forced to return home he assumed that task alone and has continued to do a great work through the years.

We can smile, now, at our frustrations and doubts of those early days and realize that all the while God wasn't seeing a class of disruptive university students, but a group of stalwart national Christian leaders for Japan's future.

Sometimes we considered ourselves failures in valued relationships because we as Americans could not comprehend what was taking place in the Japanese minds. One of my first, hard confrontations with this was with Toshiko San.

I was particularly vulnerable in her case because I made the error of feeling I understood Toshiko San well. Most of the girls who had lived and worked in our home had come to us as non-Christians. Although some of them became Christians there, still we expected periods of rather slow growth because of their backgrounds.

However, Toshiko San came to us bubbling over with the joy of her faith from the beginning. She had been a member of Matsumura Sensei's church in southern Japan before he had moved to Tokyo to establish the work at Tokiwadai. She had graduated from high school in Omuta on the island of Kyushu and wanted to come to work in the nation's capital.

Matsumura Sensei had introduced us. It had been an extremely pleasant relationship. She was eager to learn cooking and housekeeping and Christianity. She loved our two young boys, and the feeling was mutual.

Her stay with us was toward the end of our period of language school, so the exchanges between us were quite free.

We all loved Toshiko San and would have liked to have her stay with us forever. As the time drew near for our move to our new work in Nagoya, I hesitated to ask her to go along. I knew that she liked Tokyo and wanted to be near Matsumura Sensei's church. I did not want to embarrass her. However, she began to talk of going to Nagoya with us.

"Would you want to go?" I asked cautiously, hopefully.

"Of course. Of course," she replied. "I want to go. I would like to go anywhere with you, especially Nagoya."

So we began making plans. We talked of the little maid's house we were building there, and she seemed happy. We talked of beginning a new work in a city in which we had had no witness up until this time, and she seemed excited.

As the time drew nearer for our move, I would get an occasional feeling of panic. What if she changed her mind? What would I do if she backed out? We were building a new house there, and it had to be finished, furnished, curtained, decorated, and so forth. We had an evangelistic team coming from America soon after we arrived there. I knew the vast amount of work to be done.

I did not know a soul in the city and had made no other

plan for any help except Toshiko San. So periodically I would ask her, "Toshiko San, are you *sure?* Can I count on you?"

"Of course. Of course," she would always reply.

Two or three days before the move we had most of our personal things packed, and the movers were coming to crate the large items. I went to Toshiko San's room early in the morning to ask her if all of her things were packed. There was no answer. I knocked several times more before opening the door. The room was empty. Toshiko San and all of her things were gone.

After I had calmed down enough from my surprise and frustration to think clearly, I began to try to decide where she might have gone. I knew that her best friend in Tokyo was Pastor Matsumura. Perhaps he would know.

Had we done something wrong? Had we inadvertently angered or hurt her? Surely we could work things out if we could find her and talk with her.

We went to Matsumura Sensei. Yes, he told us, she was there at his home. She had never planned to go to Nagoya with us. She had not known how to tell us. We should not try to see her. It would embarrass her, and we had embarrassed her enough already.

We felt indignant. He was acting as if *we* had done something wrong, and we felt we were the ones who had been lied to.

"You do not understand," he said patiently. "She could not have done otherwise. As long as she was your guest, living under your roof, she could only answer what she thought you wanted to hear. It would have been very impolite for her to do otherwise. It would have been like saying, 'I do not like you,' and she could not do that. She loves you and she wanted to please you. She was just trying to say that. You should have known it did not mean she would go with you. You should have met her somewhere else to discuss it, perhaps with a go-between. I am sorry you do not understand us Japanese."

We went away feeling reprimanded. We also felt confused. All of our background led us to feel we had been deceived at a very crucial time. Yet all else we knew of Toshiko San testified to her Christian dedication.

The years have borne out this latter. She attended kindergarten training school at our school in Fukuoka and became an outstanding worker. She then married one of our finest young pastors and became an excellent pastor's wife and a good mother. Her husband has visited us in the States in recent years and brought us love and greetings from her in their home in Nagasaki. He told us how much she had talked of the time in our home and what it had meant to her personal growth.

I saw her on national television not long ago. It was a special program about the interchanges between their church in Hiroshima and a church in Texas that was trying to build a bridge of love that would overcome any residue of ill feelings left by the bombings of Nagasaki. I was very proud of her; she looked poised and happy. I wondered if she ever understood any of the frustration she had caused me in those early years. That frustration should have helped prepare me for a much greater cultural frustration we were to face in Nagoya.

I have already mentioned that Nagoya is the third largest city in Japan and that we were going there to do pioneer work. We asked for help and were assigned a student who was just graduating from our seminary in Fukuoka to work with us.

Tomita San was a delightful young man. He looked

like a very cute nineteen-year-old to us. But we soon learned that he had graduated from college, taught junior high school in Tokyo, and, feeling a call to preach, gone on to the seminary. He had never pastored a church, but we had heard of him before for two reasons. His father was pastor of the Daiichi Church in Tokyo where some of our friends had worked. Also, he had worked with our national Royal Ambassador program for junior and senior high school boys and had been quite popular with many of the young men in our churches.

It was very easy to love him from the start. He was friendly, enthusiastic, and hardworking. We were soon on a first-name basis, and we always called him Keiji San.

When we first sat down with him in Nagoya to take inventory and make plans, he told us he had heard that a family having three Christian teenagers who had attended our schools in the south was living somewhere in Nagoya. Ernest and Keiji San set out to find them, and when they had located them they agreed to help us. They were the Shimoda family. Their parents were not Christians, but the three children, one boy and his two younger sisters, were valuable help to us in all that was to be done.

We were to have Dr. Baker James Cauthen to come from America, as part of a nationwide crusade, to preach in our first citywide campaign. We rented a large auditorium near the central train station of the city, where thousands of people passed by every day. We had signs printed and posted them all over the city. Also, we had thousands of handbills printed and worked very hard at distributing them. We rented an auditorium in one of the city buildings for us to hold services each Sunday. Then we rented loudspeakers and mounted them on our car, and Keiji and Ernest spent hours driving around the station area and announcing the meetings.

In short, our little team of six tried to do all of the tasks a large citywide team might do in America. Neither did we neglect to pray together earnestly for the presence of the Holy Spirit in all we were doing. We sang together and prepared song sheets for the crowd. We practiced for special music. We ordered hundreds of Gospels of John in Japanese to distribute to converts and seekers.

When the services finally began Dr. Cauthen, with an interpreter, did a tremendous job of presenting the gospel in such a simple and yet dynamic way that people were drawn to commitment, even though many were hearing of Christ for their very first time. Several hundred people came to the auditorium each night. At the end of three nights over three hundred people had either accepted Christ or had expressed a desire to know him. Some in the latter category joined a study group to learn more about him.

Of course all of these did not follow through, although we spent much time in follow-up ministry. But some of the present-day deacons of the now strong Nagoya church date back to decisions made in these first services.

At any rate, we had our nucleus for beginning a work; and from that moment on we always had plenty to do. Keiji San worked diligently and did a masterful job of preaching, leading, and inspiring others to work. In the next two and one-half years both the work of the new congregation and our friendship with Keiji San flourished. We would hear some of our fellow missionaries talk of their difficulties in understanding the Japanese mind and coming to a real closeness with their

Japanese co-laborers. We will have to admit that we felt almost smug because of what we considered to be almost a total lack of such problems. We were so sure that we understood Keiji, and he us, that we could scarcely imagine something disturbing the sweet fellowship we knew. We had a lot to learn.

Things seemed to be going along well. The Sunday services continued to meet in the rented auditorium; but all of the other meetings, prayer services, teachers' meetings, choir rehearsals, special classes, women's groups, and mission organizations met in our home.

After an intense search we were able to purchase an excellent piece of land near one of the busiest intersections in the city. After long hours of planning, consulting, and overseeing we were able to erect a beautiful church with a small educational wing. This wing also included an efficiency apartment for the pastor. The work grew slowly but steadily, and we were able to organize into a church with Tomita Sensei, Keiji San, as the pastor.

An attractive, young, unmarried pastor attracted quite a few young ladies to the church. I worked with this group, and we organized a lively mission organization. We had great times together. Most of the women had never before been offered such opportunities for close fellowship as our day camps, slumber parties, songfests, and social hours afforded them.

They were a very attractive group, but the most attractive of them was our young president, Yoshida San. She had been one of our early converts and was extremely dedicated from the start.

Several things brought Yoshida San and Tomita San together. She had a number of problems in turning from the faith of her parents and needed his encouragement and counseling. She was the most dependable teacher we had in our young Sunday School, so they had much planning and working together.

In Japan it was quite acceptable for these young church members to do a number of things for their pastor—prepare food for him occasionally, offer to clean his apartment, or even, if done with discretion, care for him when he was ill.

We could see a relationship developing long before Keiji was willing to admit, even to himself, I think, that it was so. He explained to us that he was long since spoken for and could not afford to fall in love.

It seemed that years before when he had been teaching junior high school in Tokyo, he had been attracted to one of his young female students and she to him. Nothing had passed between them at the time except this mutual attraction, but both their families had noticed it and were pleased. Keiji's father, as pastor of the church, and one of his fine members, who happened to be the girl's father, had gotten together and made a pact that was mutually pleasing to both families. True to Japanese custom, the parents had met and arranged for a marriage to take place some years in the future when the girl had finished school and Keiji had finished graduate school and become established in a profession. Since Keiji San liked the girl a lot and since he had grown up with the idea that this was the way such things were done, he had accepted the arrangement happily for a number of years. In fact, he was very slow to question it now. But gradually he came to face the situation that the rest of us had seen, that he had deep new feelings which must be dealt with.

The Tokyo arrangement was very involved. Since both families lived close together and both had operated during the intervening years on the premise that everything was settled, they had acted accordingly. The girl and her family had been kept up to date on Keiji San. They had been, over the years, preparing for the oncoming marriage.

Keiji San had told us and the other church members that he was engaged and would one day marry the girl in Tokyo. But he had not counted on falling in love with Yoshida San.

We could see evidence of the painful mental struggle he was facing and were really quite relieved when he told us he was going to Tokyo to cancel the wedding plans. But he came back to us more confused than before. He even locked himself in his apartment and for a while refused to talk to anyone. We got some hint of what was happening when we saw how upset Yoshida San was.

Finally it all came out. After arriving in Tokyo and talking with his father, he had been unable to carry through with the cancellation. He had decided to go ahead with the marriage, and the girl he was betrothed to was coming to Nagoya to meet everyone.

She was a fine girl and obviously was trying very hard to be what Keiji San wanted in a wife.

Keiji San did not attempt to explain to us. He continued to go through a long internal struggle, and during this time he found it very difficult to put his best into his church work. Finally, one Sunday morning he called Ernest in for a conference. He felt very guilty, he said, about his inability to settle his own personal problems and the ill effect he felt it was having on his church duties. He wished to apologize to the church in the morning worship service. He had reached a decision as to where his duties lay, was going ahead with his marriage, and would be giving himself in renewed dedication to the task of the church. He wanted Ernest to prepare a prayer of dedication for him to say at the close of the service.

He preached a beautiful sermon, and everyone present was moved by it. Then he called on Ernest for the dedicatory prayer. Ernest prayed a quiet and meaningful prayer. When he had finished we all raised our heads to find that Keiji San had disappeared. It took a few minutes before we realized that Yoshida San was also gone. Ernest closed the service with as little confusion as possible, and we spent the next several days trying to find some trace of the missing pair.

The situation came at a very difficult time for us. We had almost finished our first five years of service, and it was time for our first furlough. Until this time we had not worried about it unduly, for we felt we were leaving everything in Tomita Sensei's capable hands. But now it soon became evident that he did not intend to return.

All of our young people had so much confidence in him that we tried our best to calm their fears. We had much love for him and a strong faith in his real Christian commitment. We kept reassuring these young people that we were sure we would find him and that we were certain he would do what was right. What we had not faced, however, was that our idea of what was right was based on a long history of ethical training very different from his. So we were greatly disturbed by what happened.

When we finally found out where Keiji San was, the knowledge was almost harder on us than the long period of worry and apprehension. He had gone to the mountain area where Yoshida San had come from and was living with her. They lived there for the next two or three years. We heard that Keiji San got a job teaching in a small mountain school, but we did not know for sure. We never did hear anything directly from them.

We felt crushed and disappointed. Somehow we managed to pull things together enough to leave on our furlough to America. Both Ernest and I were exhausted when we boarded the ocean liner to return home. I was seven months pregnant with our fourth child, and Ernest looked haggard and tired. We were not out of the harbor before he collapsed in a fever which was later diagnosed as rheumatoid arthritis. I remember vividly how helpless we both felt to explain when the doctor asked, "Have you been under any particular strain of late?"

In America, I am aware, that might have been the sad end of the story. I am glad we were to learn the lesson that God doesn't always operate by twentieth-century American standards. Two years later we heard that God was calling Tomita San back into the pulpit. He went to the executive secretary of our convention and asked for the privilege of telling his side of the story and offering an apology to the convention. He was given that opportunity.

According to Tomita San, he had never felt that he had had a choice. He could not turn from the woman he felt God had brought to him, whom he loved and shared his faith with on a very deep level. Neither could he do what he felt would have brought humiliation and disgrace to his aging minister father. When he had gone to Tokyo to try to cancel the marriage plans, he realized how deeply his father felt committed to the arrangement. The father would have been hurt to admit that his son had refused to honor the arrangements he had made in what, to the

Japanese mind, was not only his prerogative but his obligation as a good father. He had gone back to Nagoya entirely planning to carry through on the commitment; but when he found he could not, he had left. He still felt that his decision had brought less hurt to his father because, instead of making a deliberate decision to go against him, at least he had tried and failed.

When he felt the constant urging of God to get back about his work, he wanted to bring it to the convention, apologize, and offer to take any lowly task of which they felt him capable. It was a pleasant surprise for us, who had seen many American ministers pass off the scene by one mistake, to find that the Japanese people understood and were sympathetic. They sent the young couple to pastor a small mission in the northernmost island of Hokkaido. It was a long way from their friends and families, but they went happily and did an excellent work.

While we were surprised at the decision, we felt it was of God. Certainly God understood their hearts, their love for him, and their desire to serve. In a land of such need, where there were so few servants of God, we were serving a God whose economy of human life far outweighed our own. I cannot say that we did not again question things our culture and our background did not equip us to understand, but I do believe we learned the difficult lesson that our understanding was not always necessary for God to do his work. The Tomita Senseis have done outstanding work for God wherever he has sent them throughout the years. Several times mutual friends have brought us word of the gratitude they still feel for the early years we had together in Nagoya. I think we will enjoy discussing them someday around God's throne.

I said earlier that we had to learn that we are not responsible for the results of our ministry, only for obeying. One of the commonest mistakes we made was to become discouraged and feel that there were no results just because they were not immediately visible.

In an earlier chapter I told of our encounter with Sumiko San, the confused orphan girl who lived across the alley from us under terribly crowded conditions, clinging to the urn with the ashes of her dead mother. We tried hard to help Sumiko San. We tried to lead her to Christ, to help her adjust to the loss of her family, and to come to have some confidence in herself and her potential. However, we were never sure whether we had accomplished that goal. When we left Tokyo she was still very withdrawn and uncertain, although she was trying to study her New Testament. On the whole I think we would have referred to it all as a pathetic, discouraging experience.

Some years later, when we had moved back to Tokyo, an attractive middle-aged woman came to our door and surprised us by telling us she wanted to study Christianity. We invited her in, assured her of our interest, and explained the facets of our mission work that we thought would interest and help her. Finally we came to the important question of how she had become interested in Christianity.

"It is because of the life of my daughter-in-law," she told us. "After watching her incredible love and forgiving spirit, I felt I must find for myself what I have seen in her life.

"You see, while my son was a university student here in Tokyo, he married a girl who did not have any of his schooling or position in life. We were disturbed by the marriage, expecially at his age; but we were much more disturbed by the way he treated his wife. He treated her with scorn, as if he were much better than she. He was never kind to her, even after she bore him his child. During it all, this girl has been so kind and so loving that she has blessed our whole family. She seems to be cheerful and happy no matter what comes. I talked to her about the faith that could help her live that way. She said that her faith was in Jesus Christ. She gave me this address and told me that she had first learned about him here.''

We searched our minds as she talked, trying to think of whom she could be speaking. Failing, we asked her and were astonished by her reply.

''You knew her as Sumiko San,'' she said.

Perhaps one of the most gratifying of our surprises in finding God at work in what seemed to be failure to us occurred in the lives of two young university students in Nagoya.

I have already mentioned that when we had those first three meetings as we began the work in Japan, there were three hundred or so pledge cards signed. Some persons were extremely difficult to find. Some we did not ever find at all.

Two of those cards had the names of Tokyo University students. We thought they might have been just visiting from Tokyo as they were no longer enrolled in the university there. After a year of checking out various leads, we had about given up and decided to dispose of the cards. About that time one of the boys showed up. He had not known our name and had gone to a lot of trouble to locate ''the missionaries who held that meeting near the train station about a year ago."

When he finally found us he brought us this report: "I promised my friend on his deathbed that I would not give up until I found you. He wanted me to thank you and to tell you what had happened to us.

"You see, the night we came to your services we were only passing through your city. We had been students at the university in Tokyo when my friend became very ill. The doctors there told him that he had an incurable case of tuberculosis. They said he must be isolated and suggested putting him in a sanitarium. But he wanted to go back to the mountains of our home island of Shikoku to die. The doctors approved of this plan if I would go along with him and find a little place up in the mountains where I could care for him. So the night we came through Nagoya I was taking him home to die.

"We walked out into the night in front of the station between trains to get a breath of air. While we were out there those few moments, your car came by with the loudspeakers announcing the services. You asked if we had found enough in this life to prepare us for this life and the next. We both agreed we had not. We wanted very much to hear what you had to say. We checked our schedules and thought we might possibly have time to attend the meeting.

"That night, for the first time in our lives, we heard about Jesus Christ and his love. Both of us were surprised to find ourselves believing what we heard. We went forward on the invitation and signed pledge cards. We were each given a copy of the Gospel of John. Then we had to hurry away to catch our train to Shikoku.

"During this year my friend has grown weaker and weaker, but we read the Gospel of John through many

89

times. We learned great parts of it by memory. Before my friend died he asked me to let you know that Jesus had become very real to him and he was ready to die. He believed that Jesus would 'come again and receive him unto himself.'

"We know that sometimes your work in a country like ours may seem discouraging, especially when you do not hear from people like us for over a year. But we just wanted you to know the difference one night, one message, and one little Gospel can make in the lives and eternal destiny of two young men."

8.
When the Light Comes

I am certain that one of the greatest joys, yet one of the most humbling experiences that ever comes to us, is to see the great transformation that comes into a life when Christ touches it and to know that we have had some small part in bringing the light that has dispelled all the darkness. No matter how discouraged or tired or confused we became on the mission field, one of the best remedies we ever found was to get together and talk of all these miraculous changes.

One expression of that change was given to a friend of ours by a junior high school girl in Tokyo. I remember how our friend recounted that Sunday morning experience for us.

He had been glad to get a seat on the crowded train. The big department stores were not open that early on a Sunday morning, so the trains were a little less crowded as he rode to the church where he had been working while he had been studying the Japanese language.

As he rode along he thought about the day ahead. He dreaded it in a way. When he finished preaching at the worship service, a time was to be given over to his *sobetsukai* or farewell service. This week, with language school ended, he would be moving to a new assignment in another area. He hated to leave these people, the first

Japanese with whom he had ever worked. But he kept wondering, too, how much he had contributed to any of their lives during these months when his communication had still been so limited.

As the train pulled into the station near his church, he heard all of the familiar sounds . . . the screech of the brakes, the opening of the hydraulic doors up and down the length of the train, the calling out of the station's name.

He stepped down into the fast-moving crowd and made his way up the long stairway to the street.

Outside there were traces of rain, and a warm, damp feeling filled the air. *Nyubai,* the annual rainy season, had begun.

Most of the people were ignoring the light rain, however, and were hurrying on their way. All types of dress could be seen—the traditional summer lightweight kimonos, many western clothes, both formal and leisure wear. The large number of student uniforms testified that the summer vacation was still some weeks away.

When the missionary came to the front of the little church, he was delighted to see the large number of *geta, zori,* and shoes in the entrance. Since it was the custom for worshipers to remove outside footwear and wear house slippers or to enter the building in sock feet, it was easy to judge the attendance immediately upon arrival by just scanning the footwear in the entrance.

Sunday School had already begun, and every part of the little building was being used by some age group.

Later, as the crowd gathered for the church service, it was obvious that the students, especially the junior and senior high departments, had made a special effort to have most of their group present for the farewell service.

Most of the girls wore navy uniforms, some with white blouses and some with maroon ties or scarves. The boys had either navy or black uniforms, with just a touch of white showing at the neck.

A *sobetsukai,* a farewell service, is normally a rather sad occasion. A combination of native courtesy of the people, their feeling of love and admiration for their teachers and preachers, and the warm sense of fellowship among Christians in a non-Christian culture seemed to make this especially true of such services in the churches.

As the missionary spoke that morning he kept seeing this sadness reflected in the faces of the audience—with one very noticeable exception. One junior high school girl, who had recently been baptized into the church, seemed to be just overflowing with joy. Many times during the service he found himself noticing her smiling, joyful face.

At the close of the service, when the members began filing by with their tearful farewells, he noticed that she was still smiling as she stood in line.

When it finally came her turn to speak she held out one lovely artificial flower to him.

"I only had ten yen," she apologized. (That is about three and one-half cents.) "I walked and walked, trying to find something for only ten yen that would remind you of all you have done for me. Finally, I saw this little flower and said, 'That's it! That flower looks like springtime, and springtime means life and new growth and beauty and hope and joy.' "

Then she said to her missionary, "I hope you will keep this and remember that this is what you have brought to my heart. When you told me about Jesus you brought me all of these things: new life, new growth, beauty, hope, and joy. You have brought springtime to my heart!''

As I heard my friend tell the story, I felt that surely he could never be the same again as long as he held onto the little flower. That flower would remind him of the joyous privilege we have in sharing our great joy with the world. I thought of all the lives we had seen changed from darkness and misery to light and joy because of the entrance of Christ.

Inside my own soul I prayed that just such a joy might always be evident. Later I wrote the words into this prayer poem:

The Fullness of Joy

God . . .
I want to walk with you in joy,
Laughing, singing, clasping hands,
Sharing together the worlds you've made,
The singing hills, the quiet lands;
To know the faith of buried bulb
Waiting in darkness for its burst of bloom;
To know the patience of nesting bird
Sending its lilting song through the gloom;
To feel the beauty of each new day . . .
Washed clean, refreshing, warm with light;
To feel the wonderful, joyous calm
Of each returning, restful night.
What joy to breathe, to see, to feel,
To walk with you in sun or shade!
The fullness of joy: to walk with you
In earth or heaven you have made.

The difference that the light of Christ brings into lives

is always joyous to behold. But somehow, in a land where darkness prevails and the people have no background for understanding the change that can take place, it is especially thrilling.

Many times I was humbled when, as I explained how I had seen the love of Christ work in the hearts of people in America, I saw the Japanese people take that little knowledge and produce depths of commitment I had not seen before.

This happened in the matter of our Christmas gifts for world missions. I explained that many Christians around the world honored Jesus Christ on his birthday by giving sacrificially to the cause they knew to be nearest his heart—spreading the good news of salvation abroad in the world.

A group of Japanese women talked about the subject at length.

"We have no money at all that we can call our own," they explained. "So many American wives work, and they can give if they choose to do so."

"Even some of those who are just housewives like us seem to have money of their own. Did they inherit it, or how does it happen?" one of the group asked.

I tried to explain to them that for many American women, marriage is a partnership. The woman usually works in the home. The husband works outside the home. But the money that comes in is shared alike for the good of the home and both members of the team.

"Our husbands control the money," they told me. It was not a complaint. It was a simple statement of fact.

"The only money we have charge of is the food allowance," one explained. "We get money to pay for the daily supply of rice and a small amount for each person in the family to buy something to eat with the rice."

"There is never any left over, even if we are very careful," another commented.

They talked of how much they loved Christ and what joy it would be to honor him on his birthday. Then they thought and thought, trying to come up with a solution to the question "Where would *we* get any money?"

They agreed to continue thinking, to pray, and to discuss the matter again at our next meeting.

When the day for that meeting came, I could tell immediately that they thought they had found the answer. They came in laughing and talking and sharing their thoughts excitedly. Several of them had arrived at the same solution.

"At the last meeting," one of them began, "we said we do not have charge of any money except the rice money and the little bit of food we serve with it. But *we do have charge of that*."

"Yes," another added enthusiastically. "We *have* to buy the rice. Without it we would not be well enough to do our work. But we don't have to buy anything to go with it."

"Oh yes we do . . . for our families, I mean," one of the younger women protested. "They wouldn't understand. Most of them do not know Christ yet. We cannot make such a decision for them."

"Of course not," the first lady agreed. "But we can make that decision for ourselves. We can divide the money into the number of people in our families. For example, there are five in my family. I must buy four servings each meal to go with the rice, but I do not have to buy five."

"Right!" another agreed. "As long as we eat only rice, surely none of the others can object to that."

My mind raced back to my first encounter with this element in Japanese housekeeping. I had been fairly new in Japan at the time and was trying to help some preschool Sunday School teachers plan a lesson for four- and five-year-olds. The lesson was on being helpers in their homes. We were trying to arrive at some activity the children could do on Sunday morning that would let them feel they had made some helpful contribution in their own home.

"We could let them shell enough peas to take home for the family dinner," someone suggested.

I was astounded.

"Enough for dinner? For every child's family?" I asked. "How could we afford that? We have such a small budget."

"Oh, it wouldn't take much. Just three or four pods to a child," he explained.

Then I was really confused.

"How can that be?" I asked.

Then they had explained to me about the food to go with the rice. In postwar Tokyo food was scarce and expensive. The people filled their stomachs with rice three times a day because it was the cheapest and most satisfying thing available. Then they bought very small amounts of other things—vegetables, dried fish, or seaweed, to make the bowl of rice more attractive and to add variety. If the child brought home fifteen or twenty shelled peas and the family was having several slices of carrots and onions and seaweed strips on their rice, the peas would add a touch of green to every bowl of rice at the table. The child would be very proud and the family

97

grateful.

Since then I have eaten enough bowls of rice to understand. But now, as the women discussed it, the question that came to my mind was, "How much could possibly be saved by leaving that small amount of food off one bowl of rice at each meal?"

I did not voice the question, but one of the women anticipated it.

"It would not save much," she said. "But if all of us did it for every meal in the weeks from now till Christmas, it would make a nice offering."

"*Every* meal? Are you sure you won't become ill?" I asked with some hesitation.

One woman seemed to speak for the whole group when she answered with a paraphrase of the Scripture: "We do not live by rice alone, but by every word that proceedeth out of the mouth of God."

It gave me a new concept of sacrificial giving. It was one that left me a little unimpressed in later days when I heard American women say self-righteously, "I'm going to do without soft drinks, or cigarettes, or a few trips to the beauty parlor so I can give a better offering."

I thought my group of women must be unusually outstanding. That was before I went to a national gathering and heard similar stories from all over the country. The one that touched me most deeply was the testimony of an old widow from the island of Shikoku.

"Last Christmas," she told us, "I wanted more than I have ever wanted anything in my life to be able to give a birthday gift to my blessed Lord. He has done so much for me, and it seems I have so little I can do in return.

"I prayed and prayed about it. 'Please show me, Lord,' I asked him. 'How can I make some money so I can help send your blessed gospel out on your birthday?''

She explained to us that she had to live on welfare, but her welfare help never came to her in the form of money. Rather, she simply received certificates for food or clothes. Very little money ever passed through her worn old hands.

"And then one day," she told us with great joy, "he answered my prayer. He told me to go to all of the local merchants and ask them if they had any way I could earn some money.

"I did just that. Most of them just looked at my bent old body and my white hair and shook their heads. But finally, one fruit shopkeeper had an idea.

" 'Christmas and New Year holidays are coming,' he told me. 'And I never have enough sacks to put all the fruit I sell in. If you can collect some old newspapers and fold, cut, and stitch them the way I will show you, you can make them into sacks. I will buy those sacks from you when you have finished.'

"I was overjoyed. He taught me how to make them. I collected the old newspapers and got to work immediately.

"Now my fingers are stiff and slow. I wasn't too fast at the task," she explained, "but I was persistent. I worked every single day from early morning until as long as the light of day lasted for the next six weeks.

"Finally," she said triumphantly, "I had made three thousand sacks! I was so excited. I carried them, a few at a time, to the fruit shop. When I had delivered them all the merchant counted them and then, sure enough, he paid me.

"Can you guess how much I made? I received the grand total of fifty-eight cents! At last, I had an offering for my Lord's birthday!"

There was no disappointment or derision in her voice—just triumph.

I realized that fifty-eight cents didn't seem like much to me for three thousand sacks and six weeks of hard work. But to this dear little old lady, who wanted so much to offer a worthy gift to her Savior, it sounded like a fortune. I had a feeling that Christ, who once blessed the gift of another widow, must have agreed with her.

Often in the ensuing years I have thought about the dedication of these women and their determination to find a worthy gift for the one who gave so much for them. I have thought of my own good intentions, which so often withhold the one thing he desires. I tried to put my thoughts into words in my prayer-poem:

Confession

Oh Christ, my Lord,
How often when I try to grasp
  the awful reality
  the complete abandon
  the unbelievable love
    of your gift to me,
My soul cries out for something to offer you in return.
In my weakness
In my humanity
In my plea of unworthiness
I cry out, "I have nothing, Christ, to give."
But I am only fooling myself, Lord.
I am excusing myself again.
For deep down within your Spirit whispers,
"How you lie! How you lie!

"You have much more to give him
Than you've been willing yet to offer.
All those hours and days and weeks
That so soon run into years
Which you clasp to your own bosom
To plan and work and use
But never really give him."
Then I hear your gentle reminder,
"What of the capacity I gave you
To know me, feel me, love me . . .
And yet even when you come near to me
And for a few fleeting moments
Clasp my hand,
Joy in my presence,
You rush on along your way
As if our encounter had not been.
How often I reach out to you
In quiet forest glen,
In the beauty of the dawn,
In the music of my sanctuary,
And you nod to me, and listen for a moment
But never accept my invitation
To be at one with me
At all times and in all places.
From time to time you say you want to serve me
And you beg me for some work to do,
But when I give it, that we may work together
For the glory of our Father,
You take the work and run away
And in a frenzied heat
Exhaust yourself in your determination
To accomplish it on your own."
I hear you, Lord.

I know, Lord, you are right.
If I say I have nothing to give you
I deny the magnitude of your creation,
For you created me for
   a fellowship
   a service
   a unity with you
Which I block by my withholding,
My self-centeredness, withdrawal,
The blatant egotism of my doing.
Help me, Lord, oh, help me . . .
Until I can put these all aside
And come to you and receive
The blessed intent of your creation,
Help me nevermore to whimper,
"I have nothing, Lord, to give."

Having watched the miracle that God works in lives when he comes into them, I know that I can never again be content with mediocrity. Of course, too much of the time I *am* mediocre, but the touching of so many lives that have, in his power, risen above such living will always challenge me to keep trying.

I remember the experience of Miss Aomori. That was the title given the beautiful young Christian girl who was selected to represent her city of Aomori in the Miss Japan contest. She did not win the national title, but in the course of the contest and all that followed she was able to secure a good job in a Tokyo office.

Not only was she unusually beautiful, but she had such a pleasant and loving spirit that most of the people in her office considered her to be a great addition to their staff.

However, there was one young lady working in that

office who was extremely plain. Instead of accepting the fact and developing other virtues, she resented the fact so much that she withdrew within herself and became very bitter and unpleasant. When Miss Aomori came to work in their office, she was so eaten up with jealousy that she developed an intense hatred for the beautiful girl.

Miss Aomori noticed this girl's unhappiness and tried to make friends with her, but the kindness simply increased her resentment.

Finally, one day her hatred and jealousy became so intense that the girl brought a vial of acid to the office and flung its contents into the face of Miss Aomori, injuring her horribly and disfiguring her beautiful face.

She was rushed to the hospital in intense pain. All of the office staff, in disbelief and amazement, felt bitter resentment toward the jealous girl. However, this was not Miss Aomori's reaction. As soon as the shock and pain subsided enough for her to think about what had happened, her chief concern was for the upset girl who would do such a thing. How deep must be her unhappiness. How little she must know of love and tenderness. How much she needed the Christ who had brought so much joy to her own life.

During the long days of her recovery, Miss Aomori's chief thought was not for herself and the difference the terrible injury would make in her life. Her greatest concern was to become well enough to find the girl who had hated her so much and lead her to Christ.

As soon as she was well enough, this is exactly what she did. She found the girl, freely forgave her, and shared with her the Christ who had made such forgiveness possible.

But of all the many marvelous changes we saw take

place in the lives of people when the light of Christ came in, none seemed quite as miraculous and hard to believe as the change in the life of Mitsushima San.

Mitsushima was a prime example of the old-school Japanese who had been brought up to respect strict military discipline, pride, and unconcern for human life. He had begun his military training when he was seven years old. He had had drilled into him the superiority of the Japanese race and their destiny to rule the world. He was taught a proud disdain, even hatred, for other races—especially the Chinese, in the invasion of whose country he was to spend most of his military career.

In later years he told us, with tears in his eyes, how the Japanese military system worked in China. He said that as their armies were marching into Manchuria, they would call the coolies out of the fields to become literally their beasts of burden. They would load these rice farmers down with their supplies and equipment and march them long hours as they would oxen. When one of them would become too worn and would stumble under the heavy load, they would take a sword, cut off his head, and roll his body into the rice paddies along the road. Then they would call another coolie from the fields they were then passing to take the dead man's place. The farmers would beg to go home and tell their families they were leaving. But the soldiers would reply ruthlessly, "It does not matter. You won't be coming back."

These soldiers had been firmly grounded in three things, Mitsushima San told us later: the divinity of the emperor (thus, the highest honor that could come to a human being was to give his life for the emperor); the belief that Japan was certain to win the war and rule the world, at least a great part of it; and the importance of his

104

family and his heritage in a superior race.

Mitsushima was still in China in August, 1945, when rumors began to spread about a new super bomb that had fallen on Hiroshima and, later, on Nagasaki. The military discounted these rumors as American propaganda. However, when the announcement came that the emperor had requested all Japanese people everywhere to be at their radios the next day at noon, they all gathered to hear his message.

When the emperor's voice came over the air, he not only stated that Japan had lost the war, but he gave a statement that he was not divine. He said he was only a human being like the soldiers who had fought for him. Many people mourned, bowed down in the streets, and cried. Others refused to believe it. Most of them considered the emperor's so-called "confession" the worst indignity the conquering armies could heap upon him to completely humiliate him and his followers. The soldiers felt deeply disgraced that they had allowed such a thing to happen to their honored emperor.

Mitsushima was among those who found it very hard to believe what he heard. He resolved to go back to his home city of Hiroshima and see for himself.

When he arrived in Hiroshima and saw the almost total destruction, he could doubt no longer. He could not find any trace of his family or his boyhood home. All of the things he had believed in so fervently were gone—the divinity of the emperor, the glorious future of his country as a conqueror, his place of service, and now, his family and his home.

He felt he was in disgrace, and he could think of no way to redeem even a trace of dignity and honor but to commit suicide. He took a razor and cut his throat and did, indeed, nearly bleed to death.

When, a day or two later, he woke up to find he had not succeeded, his depression was worse than ever.

"I am the lowest of the low!" he cried out. "I cannot even commit an honorable suicide."

While he had been lying near death, a beautiful young girl from a wealthy Hiroshima family had found him. She was a Christian who had attended our Christian girls' school, Seinan Jo Gakuin, in Kokura. She was overcome with concern for this desperate young soldier and wanted to take him home and nurse him back to health. She hurried home to ask her family. They understood her concern and allowed her to have him moved to their home. This was, in itself, a very unusual thing for a Japanese family.

As soon as Mitsushima was well enough to stroll out in the ruins of the city alone, an incident happened that was to affect the whole course of his life.

One evening as he was walking along the bombed-out streets he noticed a rather large group of people walking in front of him. He was surprised when this group suddenly turned off and went into one of the ruins along the street. Curiosity caused him to stop and see what they were doing.

They walked into the ruins of a church where only part of the foundation and two partial walls were still standing. In the shadow of those ruins they began to hold a worship service.

Mitsushima stood outside and listened to the hymns, the prayers, and the Scripture readings. When the service was over he watched the faces of the people as they left.

"They have something I do not have," he whispered to himself. "They still have something of meaning in their lives, even though everything has been destroyed.''

This was his first tiny step in a new direction.

During the long days of convalescence, the family with whom he was staying became fond of the despondent soldier. Having satisfied themselves that he had come from an excellent family which had seemingly been destroyed in the atomic blast, they asked to adopt him as their son. They made the arrangements for a marriage contract between him and their daughter who had saved his life. This contract had the provision that he take their family name, as they had no other male heir. It was at this time that he officially became known by the name Mitsushima, although none of us knew him by any other name.

However, the young couple, though very fond of each other, objected to the marriage arrangement. They considered themselves a part of the emerging new Japanese youth who chose to make their decisions for themselves. They went together before her parents and told them that they must make their own decisions and that they could not accept the marriage plans.

In later years Mitsushima would laugh as he would tell how, soon after any compulsion to marry was lifted, the young couple fell deeply in love. Once again they had to go before her parents. This time it was to inform them that they *would* marry, but for reasons of their own.

As the beautiful girl cared for him and came to love him, Mitsushima was drawn to the faith that motivated all she did. To accept such a faith would be a very drastic step for the young soldier so rigidly trained in a cruel discipline. He hesitated, but he agreed to go to Seinan Gakuin University, the male counterpart of the Christian girls' school she had attended.

107

As it turned out, this experience included many unpleasant duties that embittered Mitsushima San and, for a while, stood in his way of making a decision for Christ. Rather than accept charity, he was determined to work as much of his way as possible. After much searching, the only job he could find was shining the boots of the American GIs, the boisterous conquerors he had so recently fought and hated. He found it extremely demeaning that he, a high officer who had always commanded such respect, should be brought to this way of earning money. He loathed it with all of his being.

Nevertheless, God was at work in his heart, and he was eventually led to Christ while attending the university. The change was radical and complete. Not only did he find new meaning and joy; he was also filled with a great compassion for his fellow countrymen who had not yet found this source of life and purpose.

Only a short time later he recognized the call of God to preach the gospel. He shifted emphasis from the English department to the seminary section of the university.

One source of amazement to him as he studied was how God used seeds planted in his life as a child. He had not even recognized them as such until this time.

When he had been very young his father had been anxious for him to learn English, thinking that knowing the language might be of value sometime in the future. He had enrolled him in an English Bible class for this purpose. The missionary in charge of the class had insisted that the children learn a large number of Bible verses by memory. He had faithfully done this, with no attention to their meaning but simply as a vehicle for practicing his pronunciation. Now that he was a young man and a new Christian, those verses came flooding back to his mind with great meaning. He often said to the missionaries in later years, "Never be without an English Bible class. You may become discouraged and feel that you aren't accomplishing anything, but you never know what God will do with the seeds you plant in young minds twenty or thirty years later."

During these seminary days, as Mitsushima San became known as a very promising young preacher and as one of the truly outstanding Christian interpreters in all of Japan, most of us came to know him. He was handsome, extremely well groomed, and, above all, very gentle and compassionate. It was almost beyond the strength of our imaginations to picture him in his old life of cruelty and unconcern.

After he became pastor of the new church in Kobe, Japan, he was walking down one of the main streets of that city one day when he was surprised to meet an old army buddy he had not seen since the war. The friend was obviously amazed and began to ask, "What has happened to you? What are you doing now?"

Mitsushima Sensei pointed up to the hill above the city, to the spires of his church, and said, "I am the pastor of that Christian church."

"It can't be! It's impossible!" cried the astonished friend.

"Yes," Mitsushima answered quietly. "Except for Christ it is impossible."

Then he quoted the words from 2 Corinthians 5:17 which explained the miracle of his gentle, victorious, new life: "If any man be in Christ, he is a new creature: old things are passed away; behold, all things are become new."

Mitsushima Sensei held many responsible positions in

the ensuing years. After a successful pastorate at the Kobe church, he taught in two universities before moving to Tokyo to work with our student ministries. Later he returned to his wife's alma mater, where their first contact with Christianity had begun, to become one of its most outstanding professors. Many of the people there say he was being groomed for the next president of that institution when he contracted the stomach cancer that was to prove fatal.

He kept the word of his terminal illness to himself as long as possible and continued to work with the students he loved.

The morning of his final day, the president of the university was called to spend the last day with him. When that last watch was over the president noted the great grief on the part of the hospital staff. He spoke to some of the grieving nurses and asked them, "Did Mitsushima Sensei show you the way of life?"

"Oh, yes," they answered with great feeling. "He taught us the way of life. But he did more than that. He taught us the way of death."

Long before, when Mitsushima San and his young wife had insisted on choosing a way of life for themselves, he had sought to see that others had the same opportunity. On the day their son was born, Mitsushima San had written on a scroll and hung it from the ceiling of the boy's room. The words said, "This, my son, shall choose for himself the way he shall go. It will not be the decision of his father."

But that son did choose "the way of his father." He became a Christian and a fine musician. Soon after his father's death he went to teach in the university that both his parents had loved and served.

9.
Punching Holes
in the Darkness

As I have relived these experiences of my Japanese friends, I have experienced anew the intensity of the darkness where Christ is not known and the joyous exuberance of walking in the light where he is present.

My pastor, Bob Norman, loves biographies—especially the biographies of certain great men. One of those he likes to read about is Robert Louis Stevenson. He told us this incident he had gleaned from writings of Stevenson's childhood. Long before he grew up to write his famous poem *The Lamplighter,* Stevenson loved to stand at the window of his home, which was built on a hillside. Looking down toward the valley below, he could see the lamplighter moving along the side of the hill, lighting lamps as he went. Young Stevenson called out to his mother in excitement:

"Oh, Mother, look! See the man who is punching holes in the darkness!"

The story struck home to me at once.

"That is the very thing we try to do," I said to myself, "but how great the darkness is!"

Just how great that darkness is became more of a reality to me on the mission field. I saw what this darkness can mean in human lives. It can mean an empty, aching heart that prompts an anguished question like

Kato San's: "Isn't there anyone to whom mothers can pray?" It can mean trying to live a life without a guide or a purpose and oftentimes giving up in despair like the young suicides at our Amagi fountain who asked, "What can it mean, 'the water of life?' " It can mean years of empty ritual and futile pilgrimages of searching and searching, even completely around the globe as for Kawada San, without finding satisfaction. It can mean dying without hope for the soul in its desperate search for heaven, as it did for my neighbor, Sanno San.

As I recall all of these things I realize anew that there are nations like Japan that are still 99 percent in this darkness. I have to face the fact that there *are* still cities of one hundred thousand still on the waiting list for our first missionary. I remember the young contractor, Mori San, and his "little old town of twenty thousand," and muse on the fact that 63 percent of all of the millions of people in Japan live in cities that size or smaller. And yet these towns are 90 percent unreached by any Christian group, Protestant or Catholic. Something in my soul says, "That doesn't sound like God's bookkeeping!"

Surely he did not create this wonderful world of beauty and light and then leave it to walk in the worst darkness of all, darkness of the spirit. No, I remember, Christ spoke of God's provision for light: "I am the light of the world" (John 8:12, KJV). "Ye are the light of the world. A city that is set upon a hill cannot be hid. Let your light so shine before men" (Matt. 5:14,16, KJV). The New Testament reminds us: "Awake thou that sleepest . . . Christ shall give thee light" (Eph. 5:14, KJV). "Ye were sometimes darkness, but now are ye light in the Lord: walk as children of light" (Eph. 5:8, KJV).

Surely we had a light lit in our hearts when he went to

112

Calvary. That light should shine brightly in our hearts forever so that out of us should flow the "rivers of living water" described in John 7:38.

If it is truly "not the will of the father that any should perish," why, I ask myself, is so much of the world still in darkness? Why do so many of his creatures perish every day? Where along the way have we missed his answer?

His answer was Calvary. Christ Jesus came to live among men and die for men that they might have eternal life. Is that his whole answer? I search my heart. My Bible tells me that there is more, so much more to Calvary than this. I read it clearly: "He died for all, that they which live should not henceforth live unto themselves, but unto him who died for them" (2 Cor. 5:15, KJV). "He gave himself for us, that he might redeem us from all iniquity, and purify unto himself a peculiar people, zealous of good works" (Titus 2:14, KJV). "Ye are not your own . . . ye are bought with a price" (1 Cor. 6:19–20, KJV).

How it beats upon my heart. He did not die just to redeem us. He also died to possess us.

On the gravestone of one of our twentieth-century martyrs, Bill Wallace of China, are carved the words "For me to live is Christ, and to die is gain" (Phil. 1:21).

For me to live is for Christ to live all over again in me. My heart trembles at its meaning. Christ did not intend to live in one tiny segment of time, thirty-three short years in Galilee, and then to return to heaven for eternity and leave us here below. He meant to live over and over again in every generation in lives he died to possess.

I am convicted in my soul of the difficulty that plan runs into in my own life. How often I take over and do as

113

I please, forgetting almost entirely that I am bought with a price. How quickly I accept the joys of the salvation he died to give me without accepting the fact that he also died to possess me.

I cry out anew, "Here I am, God. What would you have me to do?"

I hear his quiet answer, "I have given you an example."

I *want* to follow that example. Still, in the face of such world need and my own self-centered life, I must face the central issue and ask myself anew, "How Christlike is my life in this area?" Many other questions come tumbling in.

How Christlike is my concern? Christ's concern was never a sporadic thing. It wasn't seasonal. It didn't vary in its intensity. It was the very core of his being, his purpose for living and for dying.

Back in my college days I heard Dr. J. R. Sampey say that according to our record of his life, Christ took only two things. He took a towel for service to wash his followers' feet. He took a cross for sacrifice to redeem the world.

How different we are, Christ and I! He was always giving. Why am I so grasping? He emptied himself, poured himself out unto death, even the death of the cross. Why am I always seeking fullness—full pockets, full stomach? Why am I so susceptible to the world's offers for "full lives"? He took the form of a servant and made himself of no reputation in his one great concern: the seeking and saving of the lost. Why am I so prone to be like James and John, concerned for my place in his kingdom?

My heart is stirred every time I repeat this anonymous

114

poem about Christ's suffering and sacrifice:

They borrowed a bed
To lay His head
When Christ the Lord came down.
They borrowed an ass
In a mountain pass
For Him to ride to town,
But the crown that He wore
And the cross that He bore
Were His own.
The cross was His own.
He borrowed a ship
In which to sit
To teach the multitude,
He borrowed a nest
In which to rest
He had never a home so rude,
But the crown that He wore
And the cross that He bore
Were His own.
The cross was His own.
He borrowed a room
On the way to the tomb,
The Passover Lamb to eat,
They borrowed a cave,
For Him a grave,
They borrowed a winding sheet.
But the crown that He wore
And the cross that He bore
Were His own.
The cross was His own.

I know that these were his symbols, a crown of thorns

and a cross. Both testify for his concern for the souls of men. In my heart the question forms, "How closely have I followed my example today?"

As I face the question of my concern I feel like praying, "God, help me to care more. Help me to get myself out of center focus so I can see a lost world. Help me to care enough to change my life and my priorities."

That brings me to another question. How Christlike is my commitment? He gave up everything—the ivory palaces, the streets of gold—for a land where he had no place to lay his head. He left the place of warmth and love on his father's right hand to come among people who would revile him, turn from him, spit upon him, and eventually crucify him. "Though he was rich, yet for your sake he became poor" (2 Cor. 8:9, RSV). Surely he had every right to say to young men like Nishina San, "There can be no half bargain. Give me your all."

I know that is what it will take. It bothers me to see so many people around the world giving their all for lesser things. I frequently recall the experience Billy Graham related about a visit in East Berlin. He watched a group of Communist youth marching and chanting, "We're out to win the world! We're out to win the world!" He made the opportunity to speak to one of the young men and asked him, "Do you really think you will win the world?"

The young man's answer was simple but decisive: "I have given my life for it."

It reminded me of our early attempts to get the Bible into the hands of the Japanese people. The mission did everything it could to provide Bibles as cheaply as possible to entice the eager young minds who read so much and so well. It was not an easy assignment, for both

116

paper and print were expensive. We thought we had done fairly well until we found out that young students could walk into a bookstore and buy twelve beautifully bound volumes of Stalin and Lenin for less than they could buy one Bible. Why? Because the Communists had what they called "an international mission rate," which meant that devout Communists at home had paid for the books already and the students had only to pay for the shipping.

Dr. Theron Rankin once said, "We are trying to save the world on an empty cross. It can never, never be done. When we are willing to put ourselves on that cross, then the world will accept us."

That sounds like my Lord. He said, "He that taketh not his cross, and followeth after me, is not worthy of me" (Matt. 10:38, KJV). He called us to be crossbearers, but he never presented crossbearing as an easy task. He told us from the beginning that he wanted us to count the cost—"as a man building a tower" counts the expense of it, "as a king waging a war" counts the hazard of it.

It seems to me that true commitment to Christ and his teachings is the most difficult religion in the world. My friends have told me of holy men in India who force themselves to lie on beds of spikes; but that does not seem as difficult to me as loving our enemies and being willing to forgive as Christ forgave, while dying, the very people who had caused his death.

I have heard of Chinese climbing stairs, from which nails protruded, on their bare hands and knees; but that does not seem as difficult as always turning the other cheek.

I have seen Japanese commit their bodies to icy waters in the dead of winter; but I do not feel that is as hard as

117

committing one's entire will every day, all the way, to our Lord.

On the other hand, I know that he never calls us to a task he does not empower us to perform. How can I keep myself aware not only of his call for complete surrender but also of his promise of constantly available power?

How often I have heard the testimonies of fellow missionaries who have heard the same cry all around the world: "When I see a Christian, I will be one."

I have been reliving our encounter with Iwai San and the power of God that lifted his terrible load of guilt, our meeting with the disinterested university students and the power of God to overcome their cynicism and doubt, and our experience with the tailor in Hiroshima for whom the power of God overcame such bitter hatred.

Why, oh why, I ask myself, *can't I appropriate more of that power to become more Christlike in my commitment to him and to a lost world?*

"The kingdom of God is spiritual," we tell the world. People have the right, then, to expect to see the fruits of the Spirit in our lives: love, joy, peace, longsuffering, gentleness, goodness, faith. I know that I want these deeply. Whether or not I want them badly enough to pay the price of total commitment remains a question as I look into my daily life.

Something within me reminds me that there is another area in which I do not always follow Christ's example. I have to ask myself the question, "How Christlike is my confidence, my faith, my trust, my belief that I am on the winning team?"

We are so quick to find excuses. The odds are against us, we say. Thre are so few of us to win a lost world, and the odds are becoming worse every day. People are busier, more worldly-minded, less interested in spiritual things, more involved in more other things. The call of the secular is stronger all the time. Yes, the odds are against us. Yet in my heart I know that my God has never been intimidated by the odds. The odds weren't on the side of the shepherd boy who faced the giant Goliath. The odds weren't on Daniel's side as he faced the hungry lions. The odds weren't on the side of Shadrach, Meshach, and Abednego in the fiery furnace, or the children of Israel being forced into the Red Sea by oncoming armies, or Gideon as his army was narrowed down to a paltry three hundred men. Long ago I learned the words "One plus God is a majority," but sometimes I wonder if I will ever live long enough to learn to base my life on that confidence.

Then the key question becomes, If I am really trying to follow Christ's example in the matter of concern and commitment and confidence, why am I not doing more? What should I be doing about it today, tonight, tomorrow?

When I was a furloughing missionary out on deputation work, people would often ask me what I considered to be the most important thing they could do for world missions. I still feel the answer I always gave is a sound one. "The best thing anyone can do for world missions is to win somebody to Christ."

When one wins somebody to Christ with a pure motive, he becomes aware of the worth of a human soul, of the destructive power of sin in lives, of the glorious power of Christ to liberate and make whole. He knows the highest joy available to mankind, working with God in his redemptive purposes. To win one man makes him concerned for all men. It puts life in the proper perspective.

I believe these things with all my heart, yet I do not always practice them. I do not work at it as diligently here in my homeland as I did on the mission field. I do not ask God every day to make opportunities for me to witness. I do not ache as much for the lost neighbors on my street in Nashville as I did for those in Tokyo and Nagoya.

I do not really know why. I do not believe missions is a matter of geography. Missions is a matter of following our Lord's command to every follower, not just a chosen few, to go and tell, whether next door or across the world. I pray God to help me feel just as responsible either way.

It amazes me that anyone could live for sixteen years on the mission field, come to really know what prayer means to missions, and ever again neglect to utilize the power and the privilege of supporting the cause of Christ around the world in this way.

One of the greatest joys I have ever known was to be on our denominational prayer calender for missionaries every year on my birthday. What a special day that became. With a great chain of prayer welling up for me all the way around the globe, that meant that for almost two days thousands of people somewhere were offering up prayers in my behalf before the throne of grace. Birthdays became like no other day. I never wanted to waste time celebrating in all the usual ways—special dinner, picnic, party. That could come later, if desired. On birthdays we tried to do all the impossible things we had been having trouble with before—that contact we had not been able to make, the letter we couldn't seem to write, the speech we had not been able to prepare. All of them were made possible on this day. After illness forced us to return to the United States, I think there is little about missionary life I miss more than this. Every birthday leaves me feeling a little lonely and longing for that great well of potential power secured for me by the prayers of so many people.

Of course, in a less concentrated manner, we leaned heavily on prayer support the whole year round. Many letters came, saying, "I am praying for you." But the promises we counted on most were the ones that came, saying, "I have set aside this specific time every day so that you can know you are being remembered in prayer at that time."

Several times I shared with other missionary friends my feeling that Grace Noll Crowell had expressed my precise experience in her poem "Someone Had Prayed." Each time my friends echoed the feelings as their own.

The day was long,
The burden I had borne seemed heavier than I could
  longer bear,
And then it lifted.
I did not know someone had knelt in prayer,
Had taken me to God that very hour
And asked the easing of my load and He,
In infinite compassion,
Had then stooped down and taken it from me.
We cannot tell how often as we pray
For some bewildered one, hurt and distressed
The answer comes, but often times those hearts
Find sudden peace and rest.
Someone had prayed, and faith, the reaching hand,

Took hold of God and brought Him down that day.
So many, many hearts have need of prayer,
Oh, let us pray!

Many times as I went around the country speaking, well-meaning people would say to me, "I can't do anything but pray." I could not help responding, "Don't say that! Praying is the most important thing you can do."

Prayer is not a substitute for service. It is not even just a preparation for service. It *is* service—one of the greatest services of all. Not everyone is equipped for this service. Real prayer springs from spiritual depth. It is deeply sincere. It is persistent and consistent. Not everyone is willing to pay the price.

Prayer proved to be one of the most effective tools of service in Japan. I never became, in all those years, completely confident in the Japanese language. So some of my usual avenues of service were weakened. In a way that was a blessing in disguise, for I was forced to rely more heavily on prayer. After we had built our mission house in Japan, one of the huge Tokyo banks put up a large number of many-storied apartment buildings just behind our mission compound. The families of the bank officials lived in these apartments. Each apartment had a small porch from which the families could look down on our compound, so most of them were well aware of our presence. In fact, a large percentage of the women's Bible class which met in my living room came from these apartments. A fine Japanese Christian lady, Tsuchida San, taught the class. I played the piano, served the tea and cookies, cared for their young children, and so forth.

However, the most effective way I found to serve the group was to keep a prayer list of their names and their needs. I made a *yakusoku* (agreement, covenant) with each member that I would arise at five o'clock, an hour before the first of them was awake, and pray for them each day. That way, when they opened their eyes to whatever the day might bring, they knew that someone had already been praying for their needs. Not only was it something they seemed to appreciate deeply, but it led many of them to try to live their lives during the day in light of those prayers.

I was often asked what kind of prayer we should pray for the missionaries, what their greatest needs were. They are the same as the greatest needs of Christians everywhere. To me they are fivefold. I need to pray for spiritual power to do the humanly impossible; for Christ-like love to reach the unlovely and the unloving; for physical strength to do the unending tasks; for patience to do the tedious assignments, whether or not their total worth is understood; and for moral courage to face the inevitable onslaught of the forces of evil.

One of the obvious things I can do for world missions is one that I didn't particularly like to talk about when I went before churches to speak about missions. That is the matter of financial support for missions. I was aware of its importance. I had sat in on too many mission meetings where we had cut requests, studied the needs, and cut again, then sent them back to a committee to see if they could be cut some more. We were not denying the needs or the validity of the requests; we were just trying to be realistic. We knew the fact: World giving never measures up to world need. Our denomination has a phenomenal record for its increased giving to world missions in recent years; but when we accept the scriptural interpretation that the field is the world, giving still lags behind need.

Why, then, did I hesitate to mention monetary support? Because I ran into so many Christians who wanted to substitute this for accepting their responsibility to Christ's commission. Too many had rather give than live. Too many had rather pay than pray.

I was right. Giving of our resources is not a *substitute* for vital Christian living. But what I was not recognizing and since have learned is that giving of our resources is often *evidence* of vital Christian living. The person who lives as Christ lives will love as Christ loves. When that love for the souls of men becomes enough like Christ's, it will be backed up as he backed it up—by giving all.

This is the only kind of giving Christ glorified. He never bragged on people for giving the tithe. He assumed they would do this, even the most legalistic of them, for it was the law. His praise was for the destitute widow who gave, out of her want, all that she had.

I will never forget the Japanese widow who spent those long weeks making the three thousand sacks for her offering. I won't forget the wives who did without all of their food except rice in order to give to missions.

I have had similar experiences in America. I remember the seminary years. Ten young ministerial students were in what we all referred to as "the mole hole" because the conditions were crowded and more primitive than most of the housing. But these ten boys, although they had difficulty even staying in school, managed to give one thousand dollars for our annual Christmas offering for world missions. The other seminary students were so challenged by this offering that, out of their very limited circumstances, they raised thirty-five thousand dollars. How did they do it? By various sacrifices. I remember that a number of them sold their blood. Another large group agreed to eat only one meal a day. Many students gave up their trip home for the holidays. Sacrificial giving. We don't hear too much about it these days.

Back then, though we were both graduate students and had two small boys and no mode of transportation but the public buses, we had a strict rule: All of our Christmas spending must not exceed our gift to Christ on his birthday. But times have changed. Our family has enlarged to include five children and five grandchildren, with three kids still in school, and we have gradually revised our rule. Now we say that no one person shall receive more than our gift to Christ. That is quite a different story. Why did we change? Demands are greater, but so is our income. We have a better home, and we drive two cars.

When have I really given sacrificially? It is a question I must face before I can protest how vigorously I care about world missions.

As I pray to God to increase my concern, I need to consider whether I am willing to go where he says, do what he commands, and give as he prompts me. The hymn *Ready* was once one of my favorites. I liked to sing, "Ready to go, ready to stay, ready my place to fill." I liked to sing it because I was certain I was "ready to go." But I have to admit that since being forced to return from the mission field I have trouble with the tears on that song. I have more trouble singing the "ready to stay" than I ever had with the rest of it. I have to be just as willing to be sent to Jeffery Drive, Nashville, Tennessee, as to any other place. Someone has said that any prayer we are not willing for God to use *us* to answer is not a worthy prayer. I believe that.

In all of these musings about my Christlikeness, or lack of it, in areas of concern, commitment, and confidence, one thing has hit me with quite an impact. If I were *really* at one with Christ, Christ in me and I in him—if for me to live really *did* mean for Christ to live all over again in me—then all of this would not be a problem. I have put this truth into a prayer sonnet:

Why do I stumble through each passing day,
Seeking priorities, doubting my choice
As if I had, alone, to find the way—
As if we were not one, and that your voice
Is trying to be heard within my breast?
You never hesitate or doubt the cause
For which we live, nor ever have to test
The goal, the meaning. God, help me to pause
At the dawning of each new day, feel anew
That I am yours and you are mine. And so
This longing in your heart becomes my fate.
Oh joy unsearchable, to share with you
Your servitude, your love, your cross to know!
Prod me. Nor ever let me hesitate.

As one of my missionary friends read one of the stories I have written she remarked, ''All of the pathos of this story is just as real to you today as it was when you told it to me twelve years ago in Tokyo right after it had happened.''

She is right. I believe they will all be just as real to me the day I die. I pray God will help me use them to keep my own mission forever, and that of others, alive.

For this reason I want to remember the hearbreak and the need. But I want to remember the triumphs, too. I want to remember that our God is able to make all of the difference.

126

When I remember Sanno San dying without knowledge of the way to heaven, I want to remember the joy and peace of Suzuki San as she went to join her shepherd. When I remember Kato San and the empty, aching hearts, I want to remember the junior high school girl who said, "Christ has brought springtime into my heart!" When I remember Hirano San with his dead, lost son in his arms, I want to remember Mitsushima Sensei as he looks down from heaven today at his university and says, "This, my son, chose God." When I remember the young suicides at Amagi's gate, I want to remember the hopeless young girl in the insurance company who stayed for one last meeting and met the Lord of life.

Yes, I want to remember the pain so that I may always act upon it. I want to remember the victories so that I may have faith that such action is eternally worthwhile.

Many challenges from many sources have had a part in my deep feelings about my responsibility to God and the world he wants to redeem. None of these has meant more to me over a long period of time than a story Dr. Joseph Underwood related to me. He told of a doctor who was in a terrible train wreck on a dark night. After the initial impact, when he determined that he was only shaken up himself and not badly injured, he climbed out of the wreckage and began to walk around among the many injured in the tangled ruins. Everywhere about him he heard pitiful cries for help. Everywhere he looked he saw badly injured people who needed help—more help than he could possibly give them with his bare hands.

He kept stumbling through the darkness and misery, mumbling to himself, "Oh, if I only had my instruments! Oh, if I only had my instruments!"

Dr. Underwood compared the doctor to God as he

looks at his torn, lost world. He loves them so, and he desires to do so much for them. But he is limited. He has seen fit to limit himself in his work by only two things: the free choice of men to receive or reject help, and the depth of commitment of those he has redeemed and commanded.

"O God," I cry with Francis of Assisi, "Let me be an instrument of thy peace!"

With a sense of renewed dedication I have penned one final prayer:

Oh, God.
Let me stand at the window of heaven with you,
And see with your eyes,
And feel with your heart,
As we look out on this struggling world.
Let me see men blindly searching.
Let me feel the agony of their cries.
Let their loneliness pierce my soul.
Let me know the hunger
Of their bodies and their hearts.
Let me remember anew
What it is like without you.
Thrust into my soul
The burning love
That took you to Calvary.
And when my heart is broken
And I want nothing more
Than to be used of you—
Then take me, Lord,
And show me what to do.
Today. Tonight.
Right now.